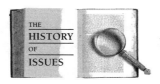

THE
HISTORY
OF
ISSUES

Genetic Engineering

THE
HISTORY
OF
ISSUES

Genetic Engineering

Mikko Canini, *Book Editor*

Bruce Glassman, *Vice President*
Bonnie Szumski, *Publisher*
Helen Cothran, *Managing Editor*

GREENHAVEN PRESS
An imprint of Thomson Gale, a part of The Thomson Corporation

THOMSON

™

GALE

Detroit • New York • San Francisco • San Diego • New Haven, Conn.
Waterville, Maine • London • Munich

Cover credit: © Jim Richardson/CORBIS. A researcher checks the progress of genetically modified rice plants.

LIBRARY OF CONGRESS CATALOGING-IN-PUBLICATION DATA

Genetic engineering / Mikko Canini, book editor.
    p. cm. — (The history of issues)
    Includes bibliographical references and index.
    ISBN 0-7377-1907-9 (lib. : alk. paper)
        1. Genetic engineering—History. I. Canini, Mikko. II. Series.
    QH442.G44313 2006
    660.6'5'09—dc22   2005050241

Printed in the United States of America

Contents

modified foods would only raise concerns that these perfectly safe foods are harmful.

Chapter 2: Engineered Animals

agency defends its decision to grant patents for genetically modified genes.

Chapter 3: Engineered Humans

ing stem cell lines is hampering efforts to combat human diseases.

Chapter 4: Cloning

\

Foreword

In the 1940s, at the height of the Holocaust, Jews struggled to create a nation of their own in Palestine, a region of the Middle East that at the time was controlled by Britain. The British had placed limits on Jewish immigration to Palestine, hampering efforts to provide refuge to Jews fleeing the Holocaust. In response to this and other British policies, an underground Jewish resistance group called Irgun began carrying out terrorist attacks against British targets in Palestine, including immigration, intelligence, and police offices. Most famously, the group bombed the King David Hotel in Jerusalem, the site of a British military headquarters. Although the British were warned well in advance of the attack, they failed to evacuate the building. As a result, ninety-one people were killed (including fifteen Jews) and forty-five were injured.

Early in the twentieth century, Ireland, which had long been under British rule, was split into two countries. The south, populated mostly by Catholics, eventually achieved independence and became the Republic of Ireland. Northern Ireland, mostly Protestant, remained under British control. Catholics in both the north and south opposed British control of the north, and the Irish Republican Army (IRA) sought unification of Ireland as an independent nation. In 1969, the IRA split into two factions. A new radical wing, the Provisional IRA, was created and soon undertook numerous terrorist bombings and killings throughout Northern Ireland, the Republic of Ireland, and even in England. One of its most notorious attacks was the 1974 bombing of a Birmingham, England, bar that killed nineteen people.

In the mid-1990s, an Islamic terrorist group called al Qaeda began carrying out terrorist attacks against American targets overseas. In communications to the media, the organization listed several complaints against the United States. It generally opposed all U.S. involvement and presence in the Middle East. It particularly objected to the presence of U.S. troops in Saudi Arabia, which is the home of several Islamic holy sites. And it strongly condemned the United States for supporting the nation of Israel, which it claimed was an oppressor of Muslims. In 1998 al Qaeda's leaders issued a fatwa (a religious legal statement) calling for Muslims to kill Americans. Al Qaeda acted on this order many times—most memorably on September 11, 2001, when it attacked the World Trade Center and the Pentagon, killing nearly three thousand people.

These three groups—Irgun, the Provisional IRA, and al Qaeda—have achieved varied results. Irgun's terror campaign contributed to Britain's decision to pull out of Palestine and to support the creation of Israel in 1948. The Provisional IRA's tactics kept pressure on the British, but they also alienated many would-be supporters of independence for Northern Ireland. Al Qaeda's attacks provoked a strong U.S. military response but did not lessen America's involvement in the Middle East nor weaken its support of Israel. Despite these different results, the means and goals of these groups were similar. Although they emerged in different parts of the world during different eras and in support of different causes, all three had one thing in common: They all used clandestine violence to undermine a government they deemed oppressive or illegitimate.

The destruction of oppressive governments is not the only goal of terrorism. For example, terror is also used to minimize dissent in totalitarian regimes and to promote extreme ideologies. However, throughout history the motivations of terrorists have been remarkably similar, proving the old adage that "the more things change, the more they remain the same." Arguments for and against terrorism thus boil down to the same set of universal arguments regardless of the age: Some argue that terrorism is justified to change (or, in the case of state terror, to maintain) the prevailing political order; others respond that terrorism is inhumane and unacceptable under any circumstances. These basic views transcend time and place.

Similar fundamental arguments apply to other controversial social issues. For instance, arguments over the death penalty have always featured competing views of justice. Scholars cite biblical texts to claim that a person who takes a life must forfeit his or her life, while others cite religious doctrine to support their view that only God can take a human life. These arguments have remained essentially the same throughout the centuries. Likewise, the debate over euthanasia has persisted throughout the history of Western civilization. Supporters argue that it is compassionate to end the suffering of the dying by hastening their impending death; opponents insist that it is society's duty to make the dying as comfortable as possible as death takes its natural course.

Greenhaven Press's The History of Issues series illustrates this constancy of arguments surrounding major social issues. Each volume in the series focuses on one issue—including terrorism, the death penalty, and euthanasia—and examines how the debates have both evolved and remained essentially the same over the years. Primary documents such as newspaper articles, speeches, and government reports illuminate historical developments and offer perspectives from throughout history. Secondary sources provide overviews and commentaries from a more contemporary perspective. An introduction begins each anthology and supplies essential context and background. An annotated table of contents, chronology, and index allow for easy reference, and a bibliography and list of organizations to contact point to additional sources of information on the book's topic. With these features, The History of Issues series permits readers to glimpse both the historical and contemporary dimensions of humanity's most pressing and controversial social issues.

Introduction

The products of genetic engineering surround us. If you eat corn, fry with canola oil, drink milk or soda, you already consume genetically modified products. Diabetes patients are treated with insulin produced by genetically engineered bacteria, the same process that produces the human growth hormone used to treat inherited dwarfism. Genetically modified animals are used regularly in medical research, and at your local pet shop, five dollars will buy you a GloFish, an engineered zebra fish that glows fluorescent. And there is more to come. Scientists predict that soon there will be animals that grow human organs for transplantion, produce drugs in their milk, or provide leaner meat. One day, humans themselves may be engineered to resist disease.

In the half century since James Watson and Francis Crick deduced the double helix structure of DNA, genetic engineering has developed at an astonishing rate. Although some genetic research is motivated by a combination of beneficence and scientific curiosity, this accelerated technological development has largely been spurred on by the vast economic potential of genetic engineering. While intense investment by the burgeoning biotechnology industry has greatly increased scientific knowledge, it has also led to concerns that advances will occur before their long-term effects can be identified and, if need be, mitigated. The beginning of the lucrative biotechnology industry came in 1976 with the creation of the biotech company Genentech.

In January 1976, in a San Fransisco bar called Churchill's, two men met over a couple of beers and forever altered the course of genetic engineering. Robert Swanson was a 28-year-old Silicon Valley venture capitalist with a chemistry degree. He had read about the development of recombinant DNA organisms by American scientists Herbert Boyer and Stanley Cohen, and had become convinced that the organisms could be used to produce lucrative new drugs. Swanson called Boyer's lab one afternoon and was granted a ten-minute meeting to discuss his ideas. Three hours later, the two excited men had sketched out a business plan for a company that they would call Genentech.

At the time, the treatment of diabetes required the use of insulin produced from livestock, and doctors were concerned about the possible health effects of its long-term use on their patients. In 1978, after two years of intensive effort, Genentech announced that it had successfully produced human insulin in the laboratory. Boyer accomplished this by first isolating the gene for insulin in human DNA, splicing it into E. coli bacteria, and then cloning the bacteria. In effect, these new microbes became tiny pharmacies, effortlessly producing vast quantities of the drug.

Genentech became one of the most successful public stock offerings on record. On October 14, 1980, its initial offering of $35 a share jumped to a high of $89 within the first hour of trading, raising $35 million for the company. Genentech was not, strictly speaking, the first biotechnology company (it was preceded by Cetus, founded in 1971), but its rapid success proved the economic potential of genetic engineering and ultimately spurred the establishment of an entire industry. There are currently more than 1,500 biotechnology companies in the United States alone.

The Patenting of Life

Shortly after the creation of Genentech, another event occurred that also paved the way for scientists to make a great deal of money pursuing genetic engineering. Indian microbiologist Ananda Mohan Chakrabarty was a researcher with General Electric in the early 1970s when he engineered an oil-digesting bacterium that he hoped could be used to neutralize large oil spills. In an unprecedented move, General Electric and Chakrabarty applied for a U.S. patent on the *Pseudomonas* bacterium. The patent application was ultimately rejected by the U.S. Patent and Trademark Office (PTO) on the grounds that life-forms, or "products of nature," were not patentable. The case (*Diamond v. Chakrabarty*) went to court, and on June 16, 1980, the Supreme Court ruled that Chakrabarty's bacterium was not a product of nature but an invention and was therefore patentable. By extending the definition of property in this way, the Supreme Court's 1980 ruling effectively created a new field for economic exploitation.

The controversy over life patents became more intense during the 1990s, after a number of private companies were successful in securing patents on human genes or gene fragments. According to the PTO, the isolated, sequenced gene is not something that occurs in nature and is therefore patentable. While patents do not grant literal ownership of a gene, they do bestow the right to prevent others from using the gene for commercial purposes. This means that any research or institution that wants to use or develop technologies based on a patented gene must first pay royalty fees to the patent-holder. While some argue that these fees ultimately restrict the development of life-saving technologies, others argue that the financial benefits of life patents encourage research that might otherwise be left undone. As American geneticist Craig Venter has said, "If you have a disease, you'd better hope someone patents the gene for it."[1]

A controversial February 2000 patent secured by American biotech firm Human Genome Sciences underscored the problems inherent in gene patenting. When the company first isolated and applied for a patent on gene CCR5 in 1995, it was unaware of the role the gene played in the transmission of AIDS, a discovery that was made the following year by a team from the National Institutes of Health. But because Human Genome Sciences could claim intellectual property rights over the gene, it received the patent and stood to profit from any medical advances made with the gene. It was precisely this prospect, that isolated genes might be economically lucrative, that was driving companies to begin submitting patent claims as quickly as they could sequence the DNA. By the time the PTO issued its final guidelines on the patenting of genes in 2001, more than one thousand human gene and sequence fragment patents had already been awarded. By 2003 the number became twenty thousand, with many thousands more pending.

The Race to Patent Genes

The controversy over gene patents intensified with the creation of the Human Genome Project (HGP). In 1988 Congress funded the HGP to map and sequence the three billion base pairs of the human genetic code, which project leaders estimated would be accomplished by 2005 at a cost of 3 billion dollars. In 1990 the project was officially launched as a cooperative international effort.

In 1991 the NIH, a major contributor in the Human Genome Project, applied for patents on human gene sequences. Although the NIH ultimately retracted the application, the move outraged scientists who felt that public institutions should not compromise their neutrality by attempting to commercialize scientific research. The fallout from the controversy led to the resignation of both project director (and co-discoverer of the structure of DNA) James Watson, who opposed gene patenting, and NIH researcher Craig Venter, who went on to form the privately funded Institute for Genomic Research (TIGR). At TIGR Venter developed a controversial technique known as "whole-genome shotgun sequencing," which used supercomputers to accelerate the task of gene sequencing. Many scientists, including Watson and his replacement at the HGP, Francis Collins, were outspokenly skeptical of Venter's work. They were dubious that his technique would produce reliable results.

Undaunted, Venter formed another for-profit company, Celera Genomics, in 1998, and announced that he would sequence the entire human genome by 2001, two years ahead of the government's revised target date. Venter's announcement immediately transformed the project of sequencing the human genome into a race that pitted the nation's public institutions against private industry. Because the PTO had begun issuing patents on genes several years previously, commentators became concerned that a private company might make claims on the complete human genome, giving such a company a morally questionable but financially lucrative monopoly on the information required to conduct much biotechnology research. Although the contest between Celera Genomics and the HGP ultimately ended in a politically brokered tie, with both groups publishing a working draft of the sequence in February 2001, the race to patent human genes had only just begun. Despite the contentious nature of the issue, concurrent developments in another branch of genetic engineering were proving far more controversial.

Cloning for Profit

In February 1997 Scottish embryologist Ian Wilmut announced that a sheep cloned from fully differentiated adult mammary cells had been born at 4 p.m. on July 5, 1996. Dolly's existence proved that cloning adult mammals was possible, igniting an international debate about the ethics of cloning. Since the birth of Dolly, researchers have cloned numerous animals. While some scientists got involved in cloning animals to provide humans with better food or to try to protect endangered species, many became interested because of the economic potential of the technology. For example, a California company called Genetic Savings & Clone can produce a domestic cat whose genetic makeup is identical to that of a favorite pet. In another instance, in April 2003 Italian scientists announced the birth of a clone produced from the skin cell of a world champion race horse.

While the potential for profit drives cloning developments, ethical concerns are acting as a damper. Within days of the announcement about Dolly, U.S. president Bill Clinton called for a moratorium on human cloning, arguing that "any discovery that touches upon human creation is not simply a matter of scientific inquiry . . . [but also] a matter of morality and spirituality."[2] Dozens of countries followed suit, but, starting in 1998, a string of high profile cloning claims fueled concerns that despite bans, human cloning may one day become a reality.

In January of 1998 American scientist Richard Seed announced that he was prepared to begin human cloning experiments. In January 2001 Italian doctor Severino Antinori announced that he was about to clone babies for infertile couples at his private fertility clinic. In July 2002 a South Korean company claimed to have implanted a cloned embryo in a woman. Six months later, Clonaid, the company founded by Canada-based UFO cult, the Raelians, claimed to have produced the first human clone. In January 2004 fertility researcher Panayiotis Zavos also claimed to have implanted a cloned embryo in a woman, but he later said the pregnancy failed. Although none of these claims have been substantiated, many commentators have argued that the potentially massive sums of money to be made from human cloning as a fertility technique for childless couples ensure that human cloning research will continue, with or without government approval.

While these claims focused public attention on the most controversial aspect of cloning, human reproductive cloning, a July 2001 announcement by the Jones Institute for Reproductive Medicine at Eastern Virginia Medical School added another issue to the debate. Scientists at the private clinic had cultivated stem cells from a human embryo that they created in a laboratory. Stem cells are found in embryos during the first two weeks of their development and are capable of forming various cell types including, for example, nerve cells that produce dopamine, a brain chemical whose deficiency leads to Parkinson's disease. While these cells can be extracted from discarded embryos left over from in vitro fertilization procedures, or removed from aborted fetuses or umbilical cords, scientists were suggesting that stem cells from cloned embryos would be superior because they would be genetically identical to the patient. Although the embryos produced at the Jones Institute were not clones, many scientists had come to believe that it would only be a matter of time before companies would begin cloning stem cells for profit. This type of cloning, called therapeutic cloning, has the potential to help cure diseases such as Parkinson's and Alzheimer's. However, the procedure is controversial because it involves the destruction of embryos. Critics of therapeutic cloning called on the government to ban any research that involved the cloning or destruction of embryos. In a speech addressed to U.S. president George W. Bush, Pope John Paul II argued,

> A free and virtuous society, which America aspires to be, must reject practices that devalue and violate human life at any stage from conception until natural death. In defending the right to life, in law and through a vibrant culture of life, America can show the world the path to a truly humane future in which man remains the master, not the product, of his technology.[3]

Cloning proponents countered that the microscopic embryos used in stem cell research do not constitute human beings, and that banning the technique could mean that millions of people will die needlessly.

On August 9, 2001, Bush delivered a speech in which he declared that American scientists would be allowed to continue research on existing cell lines drawn from frozen embryos, but no federal funds would be given to research that utilized new embryos. Critics argued that the decision to deny public researchers the funding necessary to continue their work would restrict the ability of scientists to develop new medical technologies. Furthermore, Bush's decision ensured that any future therapeutic cloning developments would necessarily be in the hands of private businesses, with serious implications for cash-strapped public health institutions, which would have to pay royalty fees for the use of patented technologies

Secret Science

Many people feel more comfortable with government health institutes—as opposed to private, for-profit companies—pursuing genetic engineering research. They believe that decisions about such controversial research should not be left to profit-motivated researchers, and have called for increased government regulation of these companies. However, others argue that regulation alone will not deter unscrupulous researchers from continuing their work surreptitiously. Indeed, there have been a number of cases in which genetic engineering developments have occurred in secret and without regulatory approval.

In November 1998 Dr. Jose Cibelli of American biotechnology firm Advance Cell Technology announced that he had combined one of his own cells with an enucleated cow egg. The cell was allowed to grow to the thirty-two cell stage, at which point it was destroyed. Had the clone been implanted it would have, theoretically, developed into Cibelli's identical but younger twin, except that its genetic makeup would have been fractionally bovine. The news provoked strong criticism from those horrified by the prospect of a human-animal chimera. Chimeras, or animals that combine different species, already exist. Scientists have produced a geep (a combination of a sheep and a goat) and a cama (part camel, part lama), and many worry that something like a humonkey might one day be born. However, what most concerned legislators in 1998 was that Cibelli's announcement had come three years after the fact.

While there are those who would argue that genetic engineering research should be completely deregulated so that scientistics can work unfettered, most feel that researchers need to be accountable to the rest of society and that strict government regulation is necessary. Ultimately, regulation may be the only way to mitigate the potential ethical, legal, and human health problems that could result from such research. The profits to be made pursuing genetic engineering have ensured that modified products have quickly become a fact of life. However, the long-term effects of these technologies are uncertain. Those worried about the rapid pace of GE advances argue that citizens and politicians must take a more active role in making sure that these technologies benefit, not harm, humanity. As pioneering geneticist Marshall Nirenberg wrote in 1967, "Decisions concerning the application of [scientific] knowledge must ultimately be made by society, and only an informed society can make such decisions wisely."[4]

Notes

1. Quoted in Richard Preston, "The Genome Warrior," *The New Yorker*, June 12, 2000, p. 78.
2. William J. Clinton, "Remarks by President on Cloning," March 4, 1997. www.clintonfoundation.org/legacy/030497-remarks-by-president-on-cloning.htm
3. John Paul II, "Remarks by President Bush and His Holiness Pope John Paul II," July 23, 2001. www.whitehouse.gov/news/releases/2001/07/20010723-1.html
4. Marshall W. Nirenberg, "Will Society Be Prepared?" *Science*, August 11, 1967, p. 633.

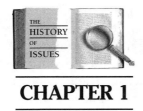

CHAPTER 1

Engineered Plants

Chapter Preface

On May 18, 1994, the U.S. Food and Drug Administration (FDA) approved the first genetically modified (GM) food for market. The California biotechnology firm Calgene engineered the Flavr Savr tomato to ripen more slowly than traditional varieties. By inserting a reversed copy of the gene that results in tomato spoilage, Calgene created a tomato that could stay on the vine longer and remain firm during transport. The company argued that this alteration would result in fuller-flavored tomatoes on supermarket shelves.

Despite its promise, in 1997 the Flavr Savr was pulled from production. A variety of problems, from poor field results to transportation issues, had simply made the tomato commercially unviable. The tomato's creation and demise had gone largely unnoticed by the American public. Despite some outcry by environmentalists and health experts, public response to the introduction of the tomato had been generally muted, indicating a trust in the government's assertion that genetically engineered products were safe for consumption.

However, throughout the 1990s Americans' concern about the effects of genetically engineered plants grew, in part spurred on by the intense controversy that erupted upon their introduction in Europe. Proponents of the production of GM crops argued that genetic technology offered the potential to reduce pesticide use, increase yields, improve the nutritional content of produce, and alleviate world hunger. Opponents countered that GM crops also offered the potential for irreversible genetic pollution, the disruption of ecological systems, and severe human health risks.

The debate over GM crops centers around two issues: their impact on the environment and their effects on human health. Recent developments, such as the discovery of modified genes in organically planted crops, have lent credence to the concerns of environmentalists that GM plants will taint natural varieties. Genetic pollution has already become an international problem, with a number of countries reporting the contamination of traditional varieties, including maize in Mexico, cotton in Greece, and soy in Italy.

In 1998 biotech firm Delta and Pine Land and the U.S. Department of Agriculture patented a possible solution to the problem of genetic pollution. "Terminator" technology ensures that a GM plant produces only sterile seeds. Although the technology offers a solution to the uncontrolled spreading of modified plants, it is criticized on two counts. First, critics argue that the "suicide gene" simply poses a new set of environmental dangers. Although crops modified by this gene do not produce viable seeds, they may continue to produce pollen, which could spread to non-engineered plants. Second, many critics were concerned about the impacts on the 1 billion people, most of whom are subsistence farmers living in developing nations, who rely on saved seed for planting next year's crops.

The second issue central to the debate surrounding GM crops concerns the potential human health impact of eating GM foods. Many scientists warn that GM foods could pose a range of unanticipated health risks for consumers, including the introduction of new allergens, reduced levels of nutrients, increased levels of naturally occurring toxicants, the presence of new toxicants, and the creation of antibiotic resistance.

Despite such concerns, scientists continue to develop genetically modified plants, so the controversy over their risks will likely continue well into the future. Indeed, unlike the Flavr Savr tomato, most GM foods are probably here to stay. Only in the future will it be possible to evaluate their long-term impact on the environment and human health.

The Unknown Dangers of Genetically Modified Crops

JEREMY RIFKIN

Genetically modified crops were first introduced for commercial production in the United States in 1996. In the following 1998 article Jeremy Rifkin argues that the environmental dangers posed by these crops are immeasurable. The single largest threat posed by them is that of genetic pollution, the contamination of the gene pool, which has the potential to irreversibly alter the very foundations of the natural world. Rifkin also expresses concern about the loss of biodiversity that will result from the development of genetically modified crops. Despite these dangers, he contends, intense investment by global life-science companies ensures that newly engineered crops are introduced into the ecosystem at an ever increasing rate.

Jeremy Rifkin is the founder and president of the Foundation on Economic Trends, the president of the Greenhouse Crisis Foundation, and one of the most outspoken critics of the biotechnology industry. Rifkin's views have had considerable impact both within the United States and internationally, with the National Journal *listing him as one of the 150 most influential people in shaping U.S. policy. Rifkin has also served as personal adviser to Romano Prodi, the former president of the European Commission, the governing body of the European Union.*

We are in the midst of a great historic transition into the Biotech Age. The ability to isolate, identify and recombine genes is making the gene pool available, for the first time, as the primary raw resource for future economic activity on Earth. After thousands of years of fusing, melting, soldering, forging and burning inanimate matter to create useful things, we are now splicing, recombining, inserting and stitching living material for our own economic interests. Lord Ritchie-Calder, the British science writer, cast the biological revolution in the proper historical perspective when he observed that "just as we have manipulated plastics and metals, we are now manufacturing living materials."

The Nobel Prize–winning chemist Robert F. Curl of Rice University spoke for many of his colleagues in science when he proclaimed that the 20th century was "the century of physics and chemistry. But it is clear that the next century will be the century of biology."

Global "life-science" companies promise an economic renaissance in the coming Biotech Century—they offer a door to a new era of history where the genetic blueprints of evolution itself become subject to human authorship. Critics worry that the re-seeding of the Earth with a laboratory-conceived second Genesis could lead to a far different future—a biological Tower of Babel and the spread of chaos throughout the biological world, drowning out the ancient language of creation.

A Second Genesis

Human beings have been remaking the Earth for as long as we have had a history. Up to now, however, our ability to create our own second Genesis has been tempered by the restraints imposed by species boundaries. We have been forced to work narrowly, continually crossing close relatives in the plant or animal kingdoms to create new varieties, strains and breeds. Through a long, historical process of tinkering and trial and error, we have redrawn the biological map, creating new agricultural products, new sources of energy, more durable building materials, and life-saving pharmaceuticals. Still, in all this time, nature dictated the terms of engagement.

But the new technologies of the Genetic Age allow scientists, corporations and governments to manipulate the natural world at the most fundamental level—the genetic one. Imagine the wholesale transfer of genes between totally unrelated species and across all biological boundaries— plant, animal and human—creating thousands of novel life forms in a brief moment of evolutionary time. Then, with clonal propagation, mass-producing countless replicas of these new creations, releasing them into the biosphere to propagate, mutate, proliferate and migrate. This is, in fact, the radical scientific and commercial experiment now underway.

Global Powers at Play

Typical of new biotech trends is the bold decision by the Monsanto Corporation, long a world leader in chemical products, to sell off its entire chemical division in 1997 and anchor its research, development and marketing in biotech-based technologies and products. Global conglomerates are rapidly buying up biotech start-up companies, seed companies, agribusiness and agrochemical concerns, pharmaceutical, medical and health businesses, and food and drink companies, creating giant life-science complexes from which to fashion a bio-industrial world. The concentration of power is impressive. The top 10 agrochemical companies control 81 percent of the $29 billion per year global agrochemical market. Ten life science companies control 37 percent of the $15 billion per year global seed market. Meanwhile, pharmaceutical companies spent more than $3.5 billion in 1995 buying up biotech firms. Novartis, a giant new firm resulting from the $27 billion merger of Sandoz and Ciba-Geigy, is now the world's largest agrochemical company, the second-largest seed company and the second-largest pharmaceutical company.

Global life-science companies are expected to introduce thousands of new genetically engineered organisms into the environment in the coming century. In just the past 18 months [in 1997 and 1998], genetically engineered corn, soy and cotton have been planted over millions of acres of U.S. farmland. Genetically engineered insects, fish and domesticated animals have also been introduced.

Virtually every genetically engineered organism released into the environment poses a potential threat to the ecosystem. To appreciate why this is so, we need to understand why the pollution generated by genetically modified organisms is so different from the pollution resulting from the release of petrochemical products [which are derived from petroleum or natural gas, such as plastic] into the environment.

The Risks of New Organisms

Because they are alive, genetically engineered organisms are inherently more unpredictable than petrochemicals in the way they interact with other living things in the environment. Consequently, it is much more difficult to assess all of the potential impacts that a genetically engineered organism might have on the Earth's ecosystems.

Genetically engineered products also reproduce. They grow and they migrate. Unlike petrochemical products, it is difficult to constrain them within a given geographical locale. Finally, once released, it is virtually impossible to recall genetically engineered organisms back to the laboratory, especially those organisms that are microscopic in nature.

The risks in releasing novel, genetically engineered organisms into the biosphere are similar to those we've encountered in introducing exotic organisms into the North American habitat. Over the past several hundred years, thousands of non-native organisms have been brought to America from other regions of the world. While many of these creatures have adapted to the North American ecosystems without severe dislocations, a small percentage of them have run wild, wreaking havoc on the flora and fauna of the continent. Gypsy moth, Kudzu vine, Dutch elm disease, chestnut blight, starlings and Mediterranean fruit flies come easily to mind.

Whenever a genetically engineered organism is released, there is always a small chance that it, too, will run amok because, like non-indigenous species, it has been artificially introduced into a complex environment that has developed a web of highly integrated relationships over long periods of evolutionary history. Each new synthetic introduction is tantamount to playing ecological roulette. That is, while there is only a small chance of it triggering an environmental explosion, if it does, the consequences could be significant and irreversible.

Spreading Genetic Pollution

Nowhere are the alarm bells going off faster than in agricultural biotechnology. The life-science companies are introducing biotech crops containing novel genetic traits from other plants, viruses, bacteria and animals. The new genetically engineered crops are designed to perform in ways that have eluded scientists working with classical breeding techniques. Many of the new gene-spliced crops emanating from laboratories seem more like creations from the world of science fiction. Scientists have inserted "antifreeze" protein genes from flounder into the genetic code of tomatoes to protect the fruit from frost damage. Chicken genes have been inserted into potatoes to increase disease resistance. Firefly genes have been injected into the biological code of corn plants. Chinese hamster genes have been inserted into the genome of tobacco plants to increase sterol production.

Ecologists are unsure of the impacts of bypassing natural species boundaries by introducing genes into crops from wholly unrelated plant and animal species. The fact is, there is no precedent in history for this kind of "shotgun" experimentation. For more than 10,000 years, classical breeding techniques have been limited to the transference of genes between closely related plants or animals that can sexually interbreed, limiting the number of possible genetic combinations. Natural evolution appears to be similarly circumscribed. By contrast, the new gene-splicing technologies allow us to bypass all previous biological boundaries in nature, creating life forms that have never before existed. For example, consider the ambitious plans to engineer transgenic plants to serve as pharmaceutical factories for the production of chemicals and drugs. Foraging animals, seed-eating birds and soil insects will be exposed to a range of genetically engineered drugs, vaccines, industrial enzymes, plastics and hundreds of other foreign substances for the first time, with untold consequences. The notion of large numbers of species consuming plants and plant debris containing a wide assortment of chemicals that they would normally never be exposed to is an unsettling prospect.

Much of the current effort in agricultural biotechnology is centered on the creation of herbicide-tolerant, pest-resistant and virus-resistant plants. Herbicide-tolerant crops are a favorite of companies like Monsanto and Novartis that are anxious to corner the lucrative worldwide market for their herbicide products. More than 600 million pounds of poisonous herbicides are dumped on U.S. farm land each year, most sprayed on corn, cotton and soybean crops. Chemical companies gross more than $4 billion per year in U.S. herbicide sales alone.

To increase their share of the growing global market for herbicides, life-science companies have created transgenic crops that tolerate their own herbicides (see "Say It Ain't Soy," *In Brief*, March/April, 1997). The idea is to sell farmers patented seeds that are resistant to a particular brand of herbicide in the hope of increasing a company's share of both the seed and herbicide markets. Monsanto's new "Roundup Ready" patented seeds, for example, are resistant to its best-selling chemical herbicide, Roundup. The chemical companies hope to convince farmers that the new herbicide-tolerant crops will allow for a more efficient eradication of weeds. Farmers will be able to spray at any time during the growing season, killing weeds without killing their crops. Critics warn that with new herbicide-tolerant crops planted in the fields, farmers are likely to use even greater quantities of herbicides to control weeds, as there will be less fear of damaging their crops in the process of spraying. The increased use of herbicides, in turn, raises the possibility of weeds developing resistance, forcing an even greater use of herbicides to control the more resistant strains.

The potential deleterious impacts on soil fertility, water quality and beneficial insects that result from the increased use of poisonous herbicides, like Monsanto's Roundup, are a disquieting reminder of the escalating environmental bill that is likely to accompany the introduction of herbicide-tolerant crops.

The new pest-resistant transgenic crops pose similar environmental problems. Life-science companies are readying transgenic crops that produce insecticide in every cell of each plant. Several crops, including Ciba Geigy's pest-resistant "maximizer corn" and Rohm and Haas's pest-resistant tobacco are already available on the commercial market. A growing body of scientific evidence points to the likelihood of creating "super bugs" resistant to the effects of the new pesticide-producing genetic crops.

The new generation of virus-resistant transgenic crops pose the equally dangerous possibility of creating new viruses that have never before existed in nature. Concerns are surfacing among scientists and in scientific literature over the possibility that the protein genes could recombine with genes in related viruses that find their way naturally into the transgenic plant, creating a recombinant virus with novel features.

A growing number of ecologists warn that the biggest danger might lie in what is called "gene flow"—the transfer of genes from altered crops to weedy relatives by way of cross-pollination. Researchers are concerned that manufactured genes for herbicide tolerance, and pest and viral resistance, might escape and, through cross pollination, insert themselves into the genetic makeup of weedy relatives, creating weeds that are resistant to herbicides, pests and viruses. Fears over the possibility of transgenic genes jumping to wild weedy relatives heightened in 1996 when a Danish research team, working under the auspices of Denmark's Environmental Science and Technology Department, observed the transfer of a gene from a transgenic crop to a wild weedy relative—something critics of deliberate-release experiments have warned of for years and biotech companies have dismissed as a remote or nonexistent possibility.

Transnational life-science companies project that within 10 to 15 years, all of the major crops grown in the world will be genetically engineered to include herbicide-, pest-, virus-, bacterial-, fungus- and stress-resistant genes. Millions of acres of agricultural land and commercial forest will be transformed in the most daring experiment ever undertaken to remake the biological world. Proponents of the new science, armed with powerful gene-splicing tools and precious little data on potential impacts, are charging into this new world of agricultural biotechnology, giddy over the potential benefits and confident that the risks are minimum or non-existent. They may be right. But, what if they are wrong?

Insuring Disaster

The insurance industry quietly let it be known several years ago that it would not insure the release of genetically engineered organisms into the environment against the possibility of catastrophic environmental damage, because the industry lacks a risk-assessment science—a predictive ecology—with which to judge the risk of any given introduction. In short, the insurance industry clearly understands the Kafka-esque implications of a government regime claiming to regulate a technology in the absence of clear scientific knowledge.

Increasingly nervous over the insurance question, one of the biotech trade associations attempted early on to raise an insurance pool among its member organizations, but gave up when it failed to raise sufficient funds to make the pool operable. Some observers worried, at the time, and continue to worry—albeit privately—over what might happen to the biotech industry if a large-scale commercial release of a genetically altered organism were to result in a catastrophic environmental event. For example, the introduction and spread of a new weed or pest comparable to Kudzu vine, Dutch elm disease or gypsy moth, might inflict costly damage to flora and fauna over extended ranges.

Corporate assurances aside, one or more significant environmental mishaps are an inevitability in the years ahead. When that happens, every nation is going to be forced to address the issue of liability. Farmers, landowners, consumers and the public at large are going to demand to know how it could have happened and who is liable for the damages inflicted. When the day arrives—and it's likely to come sooner rather than later—"genetic pollution" will take its place alongside petrochemical and nuclear pollution as a grave threat to the Earth's already beleaguered environment.

Allergic to Technology?

The introduction of new genetically engineered organisms also raises a number of serious human health issues that have yet to be resolved. Health professionals and consumer organizations are most concerned about the potential allergenic effects of genetically engineered foods. The Food and Drug Administration (FDA) announced in 1992 that special labeling for genetically engineered foods would not be required, touching off protest among food professionals, including the nation's leading chefs and many wholesalers and retailers.

With two percent of adults and eight percent of children having allergic responses to commonly eaten foods, consumer advocates argue that all gene-spliced foods need to be properly labeled so that consumers can avoid health risks. Their concerns were heightened in 1996 when *The New England Journal of Medicine* published a study showing genetically engineered soybeans containing a gene from a Brazil nut could create an allergic reaction in people who were allergic to the nuts. The test result was unwelcome news for Pioneer Hi-Bred International, the Iowa-based seed company that hoped to market the new genetically engineered soy. Though the FDA said it would label any genetically engineered foods containing genes from common allergenic organisms, the agency fell well short of requiring across-the-board labeling, leaving *The New England Journal of Medicine* editors to ask what protection consumers would have against genes from organisms that have never before been part of the human diet and that might be potential allergens. Concerned over the agency's seeming disregard for human health, the *Journal* editors concluded that FDA policy "would appear to favor industry over consumer protection."

Depleting the Gene Pool

Ironically, all of the many efforts to reseed the biosphere with a laboratory-conceived second Genesis may eventually come to naught because of a massive catch-22 that lies at the heart of the new technology revolution. On the one hand, the success of the biotech revolution is wholly dependent on access to a rich reservoir of genes to create new characteristics and properties in crops and animals grown for food, fiber and energy, and products used for pharmaceutical and medical purposes. Genes containing beneficial traits that can be manipulated, transformed and inserted into organisms destined for the commercial market come from either the wild or from traditional crops and animal breeds (and from human beings). Notwithstanding its awesome ability to transform nature into commercially marketable commodities, the biotech industry still remains utterly dependent upon nature's seed stock—germplasm—for its raw resources. At present, it is impossible to create a "useful" new gene in the laboratory. In this sense, biotechnology remains an extractive industry. It can rearrange genetic material, but cannot create it. On the other hand, the very practice of biotechnology—including cloning, tissue culturing and gene splicing—is likely to result in increasing genetic uniformity, a narrowing of the gene pool, and loss of the very genetic diversity that is so essential to guaranteeing the success of the biotech industry in the future.

In his book *The Last Harvest*, Paul Raeburn, the science editor for *Business Week*, penetrates to the heart of the problem. He writes, "Scientists can accomplish remarkable feats in manipulating molecules and cells, but they are utterly incapable of re-creating even the simplest forms of life in test tubes. Germplasm provides our lifeline into the future. No breakthrough in fundamental research can compensate for the loss of the genetic material crop breeders depend upon."

Agricultural biotechnology greatly increases the uniformity of agricultural practices as did the Green Revolution[1] when it was introduced more than 30 years ago. Like its predecessor, the goal is to create superior varieties that can be planted as monocultures in agricultural regions all over the world. A handful of life-science companies are

1. The Green Revolution was an organized effort to invent and disseminate new seeds and agricultural practices in order to increase agricultural output, particularly in less developed countries.

staking out the new biotech turf, each aggressively marketing their own patented brands of "super seeds"—and soon "super" farm animals as well. The new transgenic crops and animals are designed to grow faster, produce greater yields, and withstand more varied environmental and weather-related stresses. Their cost effectiveness, in the short run, is likely to guarantee them a robust market. In an industry where profit margins are notoriously low, farmers will likely jump at the opportunity of saving a few dollars per acre and a few cents per pound by shifting quickly to the new transgenic crops and animals.

However, the switch to a handful of patented transgenic seeds and livestock animals will likely further erode the genetic pool as farmers abandon the growing of traditional varieties and breeds in favor of the commercially more competitive patented products. By focusing on short-term market priorities, the biotech industry threatens to destroy the very genetic heirlooms that might one day be worth their weight in gold as a line of defense against new resistant diseases or superbugs.

Most molecular biologists and the biotechnology industry, at large, have all but dismissed the growing criticism of ecologists, whose recent studies suggest that the biotech revolution will likely be accompanied by the proliferation and spread of genetic pollution and the wholesale loss of genetic diversity. Nonetheless, the uncontrollable spread of super weeds, the buildup of resistant strains of bacteria and new super insects, the creation of novel viruses, the destabilization of whole ecosystems, the genetic contamination of food, and the steady depletion of the gene pool are no longer minor considerations, the mere grumbling of a few disgruntled critics. To ignore the warnings is to place the biosphere and civilization in harm's way in the coming years. Pestilence, famine, and the spread of new kinds of diseases throughout the world might yet turn out to be the final act in the script being prepared for the biotech century.

Regulation Can Ensure the Safety of Genetically Modified Food

DAN GLICKMAN

Genetically modified (GM) crops were first introduced for commercial production in the United States in 1996. U.S. farmers currently produce nearly two-thirds of all biotechnology crops planted globally. Other countries, most notably in Europe, have been reluctant to accept GM crops due to worries about the crops' safety. On May 13, 2003, the U.S. launched a complaint before the World Trade Organization to try to force Europe to allow the import of GM foods, most notably U.S. soybeans and corn. Although the issue has not been resolved, in 2004 the European Union broke its six-year unofficial moratorium on the introduction of GM crops when it approved the import of two varieties of GM maize.

In the following speech, originally delivered before the National Press Club in 1999, U.S. Secretary of Agriculture Dan Glickman argues that the U.S. regulatory system ensures the safety of GM foods. Therefore, he contends, European resistance to these products is scientifically unfounded. Although there are dangers associated with GM foods, such foods also offer the potential to reduce pesticide use, increase yields, improve nutritional content, and alleviate world hunger, he claims. In order to exploit the positive aspects of GM crops,

Dan Glickman, "New Crops, New Century, New Challenges: How Will Scientists, Farmers, and Consumers Learn to Love Biotechnology and What Happens If They Don't?" www.usda.gov, July 13, 1999.

Glickman argues that five criteria need to be met. There must be a regulatory process to ensure food safety, consumer acceptance must be encouraged, farmer's rights must be protected, corporations must act responsibly, and free and open trade between America and Europe must be established. Glickman served as secretary of agriculture from 1995 to 2001.

L et's think about this hypothetical situation for a moment: Let's suppose that today's salad was made with the new carrot from Press Club Farms, Inc. Farmers grow the new carrot on fewer acres because it yields more, and it's less expensive because it does not require any fertilizers or pesticides and can be harvested totally mechanically. In addition, it has more vitamin A & C than traditional varieties and stays crisper longer and keeps its fresh taste longer.

But, because this carrot does not require as much labor, the farmers have had to lay off hundreds of employees. While it does not require any chemicals to flourish, this new carrot does affect the environment by making it difficult for other crops or plants in close proximity to survive. And though it's cheaper to begin with, it's only available from one company, which could result in a considerable premium over regular carrot seed.

And what's the secret to this hypothetical new carrot? It's the latest advance from biotechnology—produced with a gene from kudzu, an invasive weed.

Sound far-fetched? It probably shouldn't: Remember the flavor-saver tomato? How many of you have heard of the so-called terminator gene which can keep a plant from reproducing? Today, nearly half the soybeans in the U.S.— the stuff that is crushed and made into salad and cooking oil and that feeds most of the livestock we grow—are produced from a variety that increases the plant's resistance to certain pesticides. Genetically-engineered corn with certain pest-resistant characteristics is also rapidly displacing more traditional varieties. And, it gets even more interesting when you consider that researchers are looking at genetically-modified mosquitoes that cannot carry malaria. So, what do we think about this new carrot? Are we concerned about the environmental effects we still don't fully understand? What about the farm workers who are now unemployed? Should one company have a monopoly on it? And finally, are you concerned about these issues and about how it is produced? Would you still have eaten it if you knew about the kudzu gene? Should you have been told? Would you buy it?

The Promise of New Technologies

Folks, this is the tip of the biotechnology iceberg. There are many more questions that haven't yet been thought of, much less answered. But first of all, and if you come away with a dominant point from my remarks, it is that I want you to know that biotechnology has enormous potential.

Biotechnology is already transforming medicine as we know it. Pharmaceuticals such as human insulin for diabetes, interferon and other cancer medications, antibiotics and vaccines are all products of genetic engineering. . . . I read that scientists at Virginia Polytechnic Institute will process drugs from milk from genetically altered cows. One new drug has the potential to save hemophiliacs from bleeding to death. Scientists are also looking at bananas that may one day deliver vaccines to children in developing countries.

Agricultural biotechnology has enormous potential to help combat hunger. Genetically modified plants have the potential to resist killer weeds that are, literally, starving people in Africa and other parts of the developing world.

Biotechnology can help us solve some of the most vexing environmental problems: It could reduce pesticide use, increase yields, improve nutritional content, and use less water. We're employing bioengineered fungi to remove ink from pulp in a more environmentally sensitive manner.

But, as with any new technology, the road is not always smooth. Right now, in some parts of the world there is great consumer resistance and great cynicism toward biotechnology. In Europe protesters have torn up test plots of biotechnology-derived crops and some of the major food companies in Europe have stopped using GMOs (genetically-modified organisms) in their products. . . .

Now, more than ever, with these technologies in their relative infancy, I think it's important that, as we encourage the development of these new food production systems, we cannot blindly embrace their benefits. We have to ensure public confidence in general, consumer confidence in particular, and assure farmers the knowledge that they will benefit.

The important question is not, do we accept the changes the biotechnology revolution can bring, but are we willing to heed the lessons of the past in helping us to harness this burgeoning technology. The promise and potential are enormous, but so too are the questions, many of which are completely legitimate. Today, on the threshold of this revolution, we have to grapple with and satisfy those questions so we can in fact fulfill biotechnology's awesome potential.

Five Principles

To that end, today I am laying out 5 principles I believe should guide us in our approach to biotechnology in the 21st century. They are:

1. An Arm's Length Regulatory Process. Government regulators must continue to stay an arm's length, dispassionate distance from the companies developing and promoting these products; and continue to protect public health, safety and the environment.

2. Consumer Acceptance. Consumer acceptance is fundamentally based on an arm's length regulatory process. There may be a role for information labeling, but fundamental questions to acceptance will depend on sound regulation.

3. Fairness to Farmers. Biotechnology has to result in greater, not fewer options for farmers. The industry

has to develop products that show real, meaningful results for farmers, particularly small and medium size family farmers.

4. Corporate Citizenship. In addition to their desire for profit, biotechnology companies must also understand and respect the role of the arm's length regulator, the farmer, and the consumer.

5. Free and Open Trade. We cannot let others hide behind unfounded, unwarranted scientific claims to block commerce in agriculture.

An Arm's Length Regulatory Process

When I was a school board member in Wichita, Kansas, one of my tasks was to study the level of student participation in the school lunch program. I quickly learned if the food didn't taste or look good, no matter how nutritious it was, the kids wouldn't eat it.

With all that biotechnology has to offer, it is nothing if it's not accepted. This boils down to a matter of trust, trust in the science behind the process, but particularly trust in the regulatory process that ensures thorough review—including complete and open public involvement. The process must stay at arm's length from any entity that has a vested interest in the outcome.

By and large the American people have trust and confidence in the food safety efforts of USDA [United States Department of Agriculture], the FDA [Food and Drug Administration], EPA [Environmental Protection Agency], CDC [Centers for Disease Control and Prevention] and others because these agencies are competent and independent from the industries they regulate, and are viewed as such. That kind of independence and confidence will be required as we deal with biotechnology.

The US regulatory path for testing and commercializing biotechnology products as they move from lab to field to marketplace is over a decade old. We base decisions on rigorous analysis and sound scientific principles. Three federal agencies, USDA, FDA, and EPA, each play a role in determining the use of biotechnology products in the United States: USDA evaluates products for potential risk to other plants and animals. FDA reviews biotechnology's effect on food safety. And the EPA examines any products that can be classified as pesticides.

Right now, there are about 50 genetically altered plant varieties approved by USDA. And so far, thanks to the hard work and dedication of our scientists, the system is keeping pace. But, as I said, the system is tried and tested, but not perfect and not inviolate and should be improved where and when possible.

To meet the future demand of the thousands of products in the pipeline will require even greater resources, and a more unified approach and broader coordination.

European Opposition

When I chaired the US delegation to the World Food Conference in Rome in 1996, I got pelted with genetically modified soybeans by naked protesters. I began to realize the level of opposition and distrust in parts of Europe to biotechnology for products currently on the market or in the pipeline.

I believe that distrust is scientifically unfounded. It comes in part from the lack of faith in the EU [European Union] to assure the safety of their food. They have no independent regulatory agencies like the FDA, USDA or EPA. They've had many food scares in recent years—mad-cow disease, and in just the last several weeks [of June 1999], dioxin-tainted chicken—that have contributed to a wariness of any food that is not produced in a traditional manner notwithstanding what the science says. Ironically they do not share that fear as it relates to genetically modified pharmaceuticals.

But, GMO foods evoke in many circles a very volatile reaction. And that has created a serious problem for the U.S. and other countries as we try to sell our commodities in international markets. . . .

Consumer Acceptance

However strong our regulatory process is, it is of no use if consumer confidence is low and if consumers cannot identify a direct benefit to them.

I have felt for some time that when biotechnology products from agriculture hit the market with attributes that, let's say, reduce cholesterol, increase disease resistance, grow hair, lower pesticide and herbicide use, and are truly recognized as products that create more specific public benefits, consumer acceptance will rise dramatically.

There's been a lot of discussion as to whether we should label GMO products. There are clearly trade and domestic implications to labeling to be considered in this regard. I know many of us . . . are sorting out these issues. At the end of the day many observers, including me, believe some type of informational labeling is likely to happen. But, I do believe that it is imperative that such labeling does not undermine trade and this promising new technology.

The concept of labeling particular products for marketing purposes is not a radical one. For example, USDA has already decided that for a product to be certified as organic under our pending organic agriculture rules, a GMO product would not qualify. And that does not mean that USDA believes organic is safer or better than non-organic—all approved foods are safe—it just means that consumers are given this informed choice.

Consumer Perception

There clearly needs to be a strong public education effort to show consumers the benefits of these products and why they are safe. Not only will this be the responsibility of private industry and government, but I think the media will play a vital role. It's important that the media treat this subject responsibly and not sensationalize or fan consumer fears. That's what we're seeing happen in the EU and the outcome is fear, doubt and outright opposition.

What we cannot do is take consumers for granted. I cannot stress that enough. A sort of if-you-grow-it-they-will-come mentality. I believe farmers and consumers will eventually come to see the economic, environmental, and health benefits of biotechnology products, particularly if the industry reaches out and becomes more consumer accessible.

But, to build consumer confidence, it is just like it is with the way we regulate our airlines, our banks and the safety of our food supply. Consumers must have trust in the regulatory process. That trust is built on openness. Federal agencies have nothing to hide. We work on behalf of the public interest. Understanding that will go a long way to solving the budding controversy over labeling and ensuring that consumers will have the ability to make informed choices.

Fairness to Farmers

Like consumers, farmers need to have adequate choices made available to them. But today, American agriculture is at a crossroads. Farmers are currently facing extremely low commodity prices and are rightfully asking what will agriculture look like in the years to come and what will their roles be.

That also means they have more responsibility and more pressure. And much of the pressure they face originates from sources beyond their control. We are seeing social and economic trends that have a powerful effect on how farmers do business. We are seeing increased market concentration, a rise in contracting, rapidly evolving technologies such as information power and precision agriculture in addition to biotechnology. We are seeing different marketing techniques such as organics, direct marketing, coops and niche markets, and an expansion of nonagricultural industrial uses for plants.

One of my biggest concerns is what biotechnology has in store for family farmers. Consolidation, industrialization and proprietary research can create pitfalls for farmers. It threatens to make them servants to bigger masters, rather than masters of their own domains. In biotechnology, we're already seeing a heated argument over who owns what. Companies are suing companies over patent rights even as they merge. Farmers have been pitted against their neighbors in efforts to protect corporate intellectual property rights.

The Role of Government

We need to ensure that biotechnology becomes a tool that results in greater—not fewer—options for farmers. For example, we're already hearing concerns from some farmers that to get some of the more highly desirable non-GMO traits developed over the years, they might have to buy biotechnology seeds. For some, that's like buying the car of your dreams but only if you get it in yellow. On the other hand, stress-tolerant plants are in the pipeline which could expand agricultural possibilities on marginal lands, which could be a powerful benefit to poor farmers.

The ability of farmers to compete on a level playing field with adequate choices available to them and without undue influence or impediments to fair competition must be preserved. As this technology develops, we must achieve a balance between fairness to farmers and corporate returns.

We need to examine all of our laws and policies to ensure that, in the rush to bring biotech products to market, small and medium family farmers are not simply plowed under. We will need to integrate issues like privatization of genetic resources, patent holders' rights and public research to see if our approach is helping or harming the public good and family farmers.

It is not the government who harnesses the power of the airwaves, but it is the government who regulates it. That same principle might come to apply to discoveries in nature as well. And that debate is just getting started.

Corporate Citizenship

If the promises hold true, biotechnology will bring revolutionary benefits to society. But that very promise means that industry needs to be guided by a broader map and not just a compass pointing toward the bottom line.

Product development to date has enabled those who oppose this technology to claim that all the talk about feeding the world is simply cover for corporate profit-making. To succeed in the long term, industry needs to act with greater sensitivity and foresight.

In addition, private sector research should also include the public interest, with partnerships and cooperation with non-governmental organizations here and in the developing world ensuring that the fruits of this technology address the most compelling needs, like hunger and food security.

The Bottom Line

Biotechnology developers must keep farmers informed of the latest trends, not just in research but in the marketplace as well. Contracts with farmers need to be fair and not result in a system that reduces farmers to mere serfs on the land or create an atmosphere of mistrust among farmers or between farmers and companies.

Companies need to continue to monitor products, after they've gone to market, for potential danger to the environment and maintain open and comprehensive disclosure of their findings.

We don't know what biotechnology has in store for us in the future, good and bad, but if we stay on top of developments, we're going to make sure that biotechnology serves society, not the other way around.

These basic principles of good corporate citizenship really just amount to good long-term business practices. As in every other sector of the economy, we expect responsible corporate citizenship and a fair return. For the American people, that is the bottom line.

Free and Open Trade

The issues I have raised have profound consequences in world trade. Right now, we are fighting the battles on ensuring access to our products on many fronts. We are not alone in these battles. Canada, Australia, Mexico, many Latin American, African and Asian nations, agree with us that sound science ought to establish whether biotech products are safe and can move in international commerce. These are not academic problems. For 1998 crops, 44% of our soybeans and 36% of our corn are produced from genetically modified seeds. While only a few varieties of GMO products have been approved for sale and use in Europe, many more have been put on hold by a de facto European moratorium on new GMO products. . . .

To forestall a major US-EU trade conflict, both sides of the Atlantic must tone down the rhetoric, roll up our sleeves and work toward conflict resolution based on open trade, sound science and consumer involvement. I think this can be done if the will is there.

However, I should warn our friends across the Atlantic that, if these issues cannot be resolved in this manner, we will vigorously fight for our legitimate rights.

The Forward March of Science

Finally, I've established a Secretary's Advisory Committee on Agricultural Biotechnology—a cross-section of 25 individuals from government, academia, production agriculture, agribusiness, ethicists, environmental and consumer groups. The committee, which will hold its first meeting in the fall, will provide me with advice on a broad range of issues relating to agricultural biotechnology and on maintaining a flexible policy that evolves as biotechnology evolves.

Public policy must lead in this area and not merely react. Industry and government cannot engage in hedging or double talking as problems develop, which no doubt they will.

At the same time, science will march forward, and, especially in agriculture, that science can help to create a world where no one needs to go hungry, where developing nations can become more food self-sufficient and thereby become freer and more democratic, where the environmental challenges and clean water, clean air, global warming and climate change, must be met with sound and modern science and that will involve biotechnological solutions. Notwithstanding my concerns raised here today, I would caution those who would be too cautious in pursuing the future. As President Kennedy said, "We should not let our fears hold us back from pursuing our hopes."

So let us continue to move forward thoughtfully with biotechnology in agriculture but with a measured sense of what it is and what it can be. We will then avoid relegating this promising new technology to the pile of what-might-have-beens, and instead realize its potential as one of the tools that will help us feed the growing world population in a sustainable manner.

Genetically Modified Food Should Be Labeled

PHILIP L. BEREANO

In 1992 the U.S. Department of Health and Human Services issued regulations stating that genetically modified (GM) food did not have to be labeled as such provided that an engineered product's characteristics were the same as its natural counterpart. By the late 1990s, however, the labeling of GM food had become an international issue, with many countries banning some U.S. imports because they lacked GM food labels. This international controversy sparked a renewed debate about labeling within the United States. In the following 1998 article Philip L. Bereano, a professor in the College of Engineering at the University of Washington and cofounder of the Council for Responsible Genetics, argues that all GM food should be labeled in order to provide consumers with the information they require to make informed decisions about their diets. Bereano claims that the decision not to label food places the rights of biotech corporations ahead of those of the consumer, exposing people to potential health risks.

G enetically engineered foods are appearing in stores, but the industry and government are resisting efforts to label them. However, the health effects of such foods are still unknown, and polls show consumers feel that such foods should be labeled. Labeling is justified on scientific and health grounds and in the public's cultural, religious and political interests.

"I personally have no wish to eat anything produced by genetic modification, nor do I knowingly offer this sort of produce to my family or guests. There is increasing evidence that many people feel the same way."—Prince Charles, *London Telegraph*, June 8, 1998.

Genetic engineering is a set of new techniques for altering the basic makeup of plants and animals. Genes from insects, animals and humans have been added to crop plants; human genes have been added to pigs and cattle.

Although genetic-engineering techniques are biologically novel, the industry and government are so eager to achieve financial success that they say the products of the technologies are pretty much the same ("substantially equivalent") as normal crops. Despite the gene tinkering, the new products are not being tested extensively to find out how they differ and to be sure that any hazards are within acceptable limits.

These foods are now appearing in the supermarkets and on our dinner plates, but the industry and government have been vigorously resisting consumer attempts to label these "novel foods" in order to distinguish them from more traditional ones.

Consumer's Rights

The failure of the U.S. government to require that genetically engineered foods (GEFs) be labeled presents consumers with quandaries: issues of free speech and consumers' right to know, religious rights for those with dietary restrictions, and cultural rights for people, such as vegetarians, who choose to avoid consuming foods of certain origins.

The use of antibiotic-resistant genes engineered into crop plants as "markers" can contribute to the spread of antibiotic-tolerant disease bacteria; this resistance is a major public-health problem, as documented by a recent study of the National Academy of Sciences. Some genetic recombinations can lead to allergic or auto-immune reactions. The products of some genes which are used as plant pesticides have been implicated in skin diseases in farm and market workers.

The struggle over labeling is occurring because industry knows that consumers do not want to eat GEFs; labeled products will likely fail in the marketplace. However, as the British publication *The Economist* noted, "if [American biotech company] Monsanto cannot persuade us, it certainly has no right to foist its products on us." Labels would counter "foisting" and are legally justifiable.

The Government's Rationale

In 1992, the government abdicated any supervision over GEFs. Under Food and Drug Administration's [FDA] rules, the agency does not even have access to industry information about a GEF unless the company decides voluntarily to submit it. Moreover, important information on risk-assessment questions is often withheld as being proprietary, "confidential business information." So "safety" cannot be judged in a precautionary way; we must await the inevitable hazardous event.

According to a former FDA official, the genetic processes used in the development of a new food are "NOT considered to be material information because there is no evidence that new biotech foods are different from other foods in ways related to safety."

James Maryanski, FDA biotechnology coordinator, claims that whether a food has been genetically engineered is not a "material fact" and FDA would not "require things to be on the label just because a consumer might want to know them."

Yet a standard law dictionary defines "material" as "important," "going to the merits," "relevant." Since labeling is a form of speech from growers and processors to purchasers, it is reasonable, therefore, to interpret "material" as comprising whatever issues a substantial portion of the consuming public defines as "important." And all the polls show that whether food is genetically engineered falls into such a category.

Last May [1998], several religious leaders and citizen groups sued the FDA to change its position and to require that GEFs be labeled.[1]

Process Labels

Some government officials have said that labeling should be only about the food product itself, not the process by which it is manufactured. Yet, the U.S. has many process food labels: kosher, dolphin-free, Made in America, union-made, free-range (chickens, for example), irradiated, and "green" terms such as "organic."

For many of these products, the scientific difference between an item which can carry the label and that which cannot is negligible or nonexistent. Kosher pastrami is chemically identical to non-kosher meat. Dolphin-free tuna and tuna caught by methods which result in killing of dolphins are the same, as are many products which are "made in America" when compared to those made abroad, or those made by unionized as opposed to nonunion workers.

These labeling rules recognize that consumers are interested in the processes by which their purchases are made and have a legal right to such knowledge. In none of these labeling situations has the argument been made that if the products are substantially equivalent, no label differentiation is permissible. It is constitutionally permissible for government rules to intrude slightly on the commercial speech of producers in order to expand the First Amendment rights of consumers to know what is of significant interest to them.

1. The case against the FDA was dismissed on September 29, 2000, when the court ruled that GEFs did not require special labeling solely because of consumer demand or because of the process used to develop them.

"Substantial Equivalence"

In order to provide an apparently rational basis for its refusal to exercise regulatory oversight in this regard, the U.S. government has adopted the industry's position that genetically engineered foods are "substantially equivalent" to their natural counterparts. The FDA ignores the contradictory practice of corporations in going to another government agency, the Patent Office, where they argue that a GEF is novel and different (in order to justify receiving monopoly protection).

"Substantial equivalence" is used as a basis for both eliminating regulatory assessment and failing to require labels on GEFs. However, the concept of substantial equivalence is subjective and imprecise.

Most genetic engineering is designed to meet corporate—not consumer—needs. Foods are engineered, for instance, to produce "counterfeit freshness." Consumers believe engineered characteristics such as color and texture indicate freshness, flavor and nutritional quality. Actually the produce is aging and growing stale, and nutritional value is being depleted. So much for "substantial equivalence."

The "Precautionary Principle"

Consumers International, a global alliance of more than 200 consumer groups, has suggested that "because the effects (of GEFs) are so difficult to predict, it is vital to have internationally agreed [upon] and enforceable rules for research protocols, field trials and post-marketing surveillance." This approach has become known as the "precautionary principle" and has entered into the regulatory processes of the European Union.

The principle reflects common-sense aphorisms such as "Better safe than sorry" and "An ounce of prevention is worth a pound of cure." It rests on the notion that parties who wish to change the social order (often while making money or gaining power and influence) should not be able to slough the costs and risks onto others. The new procedure's proponents should have to prove it is safe rather than forcing regulators or citizens to prove a lack of safety.

For GEFs, labeling performs important functions in carrying out the precautionary principle. It places a burden on industry to show that genetic manipulations are socially beneficial and provides a financial incentive for them to do research to reduce uncertainty about the consequences of GEFs.

Democratic notions of free speech include the right to receive information as well as to disseminate it. It is fundamental to capitalist market theory that for transactions to be most efficient all parties must have "perfect information." The realities of modern food production create a tremendous imbalance of knowledge between producer and purchaser. Our society has relied on the government to redress this imbalance and make grocery shopping a fairer and more efficient—as well as safer—activity.

Look Before You Eat

In an economic democracy, choice is the fundamental prerogative of the purchaser.

As some biologists have put it, "The risk associated with genetically engineered foods is derived from the fact that, although genetic engineers can cut and splice DNA molecules with precision in the test tube, when those altered DNA molecules are introduced into a living organism, the full range of effects on that organism cannot be predicted or known before commercialization. The introduced DNA may bring about unintended changes, some of which may be damaging to health."

Numerous opinion polls in the U.S. and abroad in the past decade have shown great skepticism about genetic alteration of foods; a large proportion of respondents, usually majorities, are reluctant to use such products. Regardless of whether they would consume GEFs, consumers feel even more strongly that they should be labeled.

In a *Toronto Star* poll reported on June 2, [1998,] 98 percent favored labeling. Bioindustry giant Novartis surveyed U.S. consumers and found 93 percent of them wanted information about genetic engineering of food.

Alice Waters, originator of the legendary Berkeley restaurant Chez Panisse and recently selected to organize a new restaurant at the Louvre in Paris, has said, "The act of eating is very political. You buy from the right people, you support the right network of farmers and suppliers who care about the land and what they put in the food. If we don't preserve the natural resources, you aren't going to have a sustainable society."

However, the U.S. government has been resisting attempts to label GEFs. Despite the supposed environmentalist and consumer sympathies of the Clinton-Gore administration, the government believes nothing should impede the profitability of biotech as a mainstay to the future U.S. economy.

The administration's hostility to labeling may also be coupled to political contributions made to it by the interested industries.

Regulation and Free Speech

The government is constrained by the First Amendment from limiting or regulating the content of labels except for the historic functions of protecting health and safety and eliminating fraud or misrepresentation.

The American Civil Liberties Union [ACLU] has noted that "a simple distinction between noncommercial and commercial speech does not determine the extent to which the guarantees of the First Amendment apply to advertising and similar communications relating to the sale or other disposition of goods and services."

Supreme Court decisions have warned against attaching "more importance to the distinction between commercial and noncommercial speech than our cases warrant." Can the government prohibit certain commercial speech, such as barring a label saying "this product does not contain genetically engineered components"?

In several recent cases, the Court has restricted government regulation of commercial speech, in effect allowing more communication. The First Amendment directs us to be skeptical of regulations that seek to keep people in the dark for what the government perceives to be their own good. Thus, it would be hard to sustain the government if it tried to prohibit labeling foods as "free from genetically engineered products," if the statement were true.

In 1995, the FDA's Maryanski took the position that "the FDA is not saying that people don't have a right to know how their food is produced. But the food label is not always the most appropriate method for conveying that information." Is it acceptable for a government bureaucrat to make decisions about what are appropriate methods of information exchange among citizens?

Scientific Uncertainty and the First Amendment

The government and the industry suggest that labels on GEFs might amount to "misrepresentation" by implying that there is a difference between the genetically engineered and nongenetically engineered foods. It is hard, however, to understand how a truthful statement can ever amount to a "misrepresentation." (And of course, they are different, by definition.)

The first food product bearing a label "No GE Ingredients," a brand of corn chips, made its appearance this summer [1998].

Some states have laws creating a civil cause of action against anyone who "disparages" an agricultural product unless the defendant can prove the statements were based on "reasonable and reliable scientific" evidence.

A Harvard analysis suggests that "at stake in the dispute about food-safety claims is scientific uncertainty in an uncertain and unpredictable world. Agricultural disparagement statutes are supposed to regulate the exchange of ideas in that gray area between science and the public good. The underlying approach of these statutes is to regulate speech by encouraging certain kinds of exchanges and punishing others. . . ."

According to the ACLU, "these so-called 'veggie libel' laws raise obvious First Amendment problems and threaten to chill speech on important issues of public concern." Consumers Union argues that "such laws, we believe, give the food and agriculture industry the power to choke off concerns and criticism about food quality and safety."

Such enactments did not prevail in the suit by Texas cattle ranchers against Oprah Winfrey and her guest Howard Lyman (of the Humane Society) for their on-air conversations about "mad-cow disease" possibilities in the United States. The lawsuit was widely seen as a test of the First Amendment constitutionality of such state statutes, although the case was actually resolved on much narrower grounds.

Consequences of Regulation

As Prince Charles noted in his essay, "we cannot put our principles into practice until there is effective segregation and labeling of genetically modified products. Arguments that this is either impossible or irrelevant are simply not credible."

Nonetheless, the biotech industry (and many governments, including our own) make the argument that it is impossible to keep genetically engineered foodstuffs separate from naturally produced ones. However, the same industries actually require rigorous segregation (for example, of seeds) when they are protecting their monopolies on patented food items.

Although it undoubtedly has related costs, the segregation of kosher food products from non-kosher ones, for example, has been routine in this country for decades. The only difference for GEFs appears to be one of scale, not technique, in monitoring the flow of foodstuffs, spot-testing and labeling them appropriately.

In Support of Mandatory Labeling

Can the government mandate commercial speech—for example, requiring GEFs to bear a label proclaiming their identity?

The government does require some label information which goes beyond consumer health effects; not every consumer must need mandated information in order for it to be required by law. These requirements have never been judged an infringement of producers' constitutional rights. For example:

- Very few consumers are sensitive to sulfites, although all wine must be labeled.
- The burden is put on tobacco manufacturers to carry the surgeon general's warning, even though the majority of cigarette smokers will not develop lung cancer and an intended effect of the label is to reinforce the resolve of nonconsumers to refrain from smoking.
- Labeling every processed food with its fat and calorie analysis is mandated, even though vast numbers of Americans are not overweight or suffering from heart disease.
- Irradiated foods (other than spices) must carry a specific logo.
- Finally, the source of hydrolyzed proteins in foods must be on a label to accommodate vegetarian cultural practices and certain religious beliefs.

We Must Label GE Foods

These legal requirements are in place because many citizens want such information, and a specific fraction need it. An identifiable fraction of consumers actually need information about genetic modification—for example, as regards allergenicity—as the FDA itself has recognized in the Federal Register, and almost all want it.

Foods which are comprised, to any but a trace extent, of genetically altered components or products should be required to be labeled. This can be justified in some instances on scientific and health grounds, and for other foods on the social, cultural, religious and political interest consumers may have in the processes by which their food is produced. Consumers' right to know is an expression of an ethical position which acknowledges individual autonomy; it is also a social approach which helps to rectify the substantial imbalance of power which exists in a modern society where commercial transactions occur between highly integrated and well-to-do corporations, on the one hand, and atomized consumers on the other.

We should let labeled GEFs run the test of the marketplace.

Genetically Modified Foods Should Not Be Labeled

HENRY I. MILLER

Genetically modified (GM) food was consumed in the United States with little protest or debate in the first years after its introduction in 1996. This changed in late 1999 when large-scale protests were organized to coincide with the U.S. Food and Drug Administration's (FDA) public hearings on GM foods in Chicago, Washington, and Oakland. The protesters objected to the FDA's 1992 ruling that GM foods that are "substantially equivalent" to traditional crops do not require special labeling. The protesters argued that consumers have a right to know how their food is produced. The FDA countered that there is no difference between GM foods and those grown by traditional means.

However, Henry I. Miller, former director of the Office of Biotechnology at the FDA, argues in the following 2000 article that the U.S. government should maintain its position that the labeling of GM food is unnecessary. Miller argues that the FDA's current policy on GM crops ensures their safety. He also claims that GM crops pose no more risk than crops developed through traditional genetic techniques, such as hybridization. Moreover, Miller argues, labeling would have the negative effect of increasing the production costs of these new products and would give the impression that there was an inherent health risk in their consumption, possibly leading to the disuse of genetic technologies.

Henry I. Miller, "Labeling of Gene-Splice Foods: A Label We Don't Need," *Nutrition: The International Journal of Applied and Basic Nutritional Sciences*, vol. 16, 2000, pp. 706–709. Copyright © 2000 by Elsevier, Inc. Reproduced by permission.

S cientists around the world are using recombinant DNA techniques to improve plants for food and fiber. Recombinant, transgenic plants were cultivated on approximately 98.6 million acres (39.9 million hectares) in 1999, up from 69.5 million (27.8 million hectares) in 1998; almost three-fourths of the totals were planted in the United States. The four predominant crops grown in 1999, accounting for more than 99% of the acreage were, in descending order of area, soybean, corn or maize, cotton, and canola or rapeseed. Enhanced traits include resistance to pests, disease, drought, salinity, frost and herbicides, as well as enhanced nutritional value, improved processing characteristics, and better taste.

The Food and Drug Administration (FDA), which is responsible for ensuring the safety and wholesomeness of the nation's food supply (except poultry and most meats, which are overseen by the Department of Agriculture), regulates these new biotechnology-derived products under the agency's official policy on foods derived from "new plant varieties." That policy, published in 1992, encompasses foods from such plants, irrespective of whether they were crafted with conventional or new biotechnology methods or with other techniques. It elaborates a scientific and "transparent," that is, clear and predictable, regulatory approach, including a description of when consultations with the FDA are necessary, when labeling is required, and what kinds of information should be conveyed on labels.

However, under pressure from antitechnology activists and their champion, [former] Vice-President Al Gore, the FDA appears to have begun the process of revising its approach to labeling.[1] The new approach, which would single out foods that contain ingredients from gene-spliced organisms, would be tantamount to imposing a huge, punitive tax only on cars that have disk brakes and air bags. The result could well be disuse of a stunning new technology, di-

1. The FDA has not changed its policy regarding the labeling of GM foods.

minished choices for farmers and consumers, and higher food prices.

The FDA has announced a series of meetings around the country, at which "the public will be informed about current FDA policy for assuring the safety of bioengineered foods [and] be asked whether this policy should be modified," according to the agency's press release. This is a thinly veiled invitation for antibiotechnology activists to stuff the ballot box and demand more stringent regulation and that is exactly what happened at the first meeting, held in Chicago on November 18, 1999. Three hundred prospective speakers showed up, the vast majority of them from radical environment groups, to denounce gene-spliced food as, variously, unproven, dangerous, worthless, unnatural, and antireligious. There were also two panels convened by the FDA that were packed with professional biotech bashers. Outside the meeting, many of the activists mugged for the cameras, staging grotesque mini-morality plays in which, for example, children costumed as monarch butterflies fled in mock terror from a figure dressed as a huge ear of gene-spliced corn.

The FDA's Current Risk-Based Policy

The FDA's current approach to the safety assessment of new varieties of crops developed by the newer, molecular methods of genetic modification continues the agency's long-standing oversight of foods introduced into the U.S. marketplace, including those derived from plant varieties developed with "conventional" biotechnology. The FDA does not routinely require that foods from new plant varieties undergo premarket review or extensive scientific safety tests, although there are exceptions. The agency has judged that the usual safety and quality-control practices used by plant breeders such as chemical and visual analyses and taste testing are generally adequate for ensuring food safety. Additional tests are performed, however, when suggested by the product's history of use, composition, or characteristics. For example, potatoes are generally tested for the glycoalkaloid solanine because this natural toxicant has been detected at toxic levels in some new potato varieties and has been linked to the birth defect spina bifida. The FDA's 1992 policy statement defines certain safety-related characteristics of new foods that, if present, would require greater scrutiny by the agency. These include the presence of a substance that is completely new to the food supply (and therefore lacks a history of safe use) or the presence of an allergen presented in an unusual or unexpected way (e.g., a peanut protein transferred to a potato). New carbohydrates with unusual structural or functional groups or oils that contain new, unusual fatty acids may require premarket approval as food additives. The other factors of potential concern identified by the FDA include changes in the levels of major dietary nutrients (macronutrients) and increased levels of toxins normally found in foods. The FDA's focus on safety-related characteristics, rather than on the method by which the food plant was genetically modified (or other extraneous factors), reflects the broad scientific consensus that, as expressed in an analysis by the National Research Council, "the same physical and biological laws govern the response of organisms modified by modern molecular and cellular methods and those produced by classical methods," and, therefore, "no conceptual distinction exists between genetic modification of plants and microorganisms by classical methods or by molecular techniques that modify DNA and transfer genes." Following this logic, the use of any particular technique of genetic manipulation should not in itself determine the need for or the level of governmental review. (However, this principle has been widely violated by other U.S. and foreign regulatory agencies.)

The Guidance to Industry section in the FDA's 1992 announcement instructs food producers who use novel plants to consider the characteristics of the host plant that is modified, the donor organism that contributes genetic information, and the genetic material and other substances introduced or modified. It also provides criteria, i.e., the safety-related characteristics discussed above, for determining whether a substance intentionally introduced or altered by genetic modification will require premarket review and approval as a food additive. This premarket review is a lengthy process that requires submission of extensive data to demonstrate the safety of the substance.

In general, however, under the FDA's policy, neither premarket review nor any consultation with the agency is required for introduced or modified proteins of known function if they are derived from food sources or are substantially the same as existing food substances, are not known to be toxic or to raise food safety concerns, and will not be a major constituent of the diet. The agency has made it known that, through non-compulsory, "informal consultation procedures" for food producers, it intends to follow the development of foods made with the new biotechnology. However, I would argue that these informal procedures are inconsistent with the thrust of the FDA's 1992 policy statements that there is no demonstrated need for extraordinary scrutiny of biotech foods and that these procedures are unnecessary and extralegal (in that they have not undergone formal federal rule-making procedures).

To Label or Not to Label

The question of whether foods derived from recombinant DNA-manipulated organisms (hereafter, biotech foods) should be specially labeled has received a great deal of attention, but the discussion has largely ignored the scientific and legislative basis for existing FDA policy, regulatory precedents, the very narrow discretion for the agency to change its approach, and the impact of a relevant judicial decision.

The FDA's hitherto commonsense approach to the labeling of food, including that which is genetically engineered or otherwise "novel," is that the label of a food can be neither false nor misleading. In other words, information on the label must be both accurate and "material," and there are only two situations in which the FDA can require that such material information be disclosed on the food label: 1) the FDA may mandate the disclosure of facts on a product label that relate to material "consequences" that can follow the consumption of a food (e.g., certain beans that must be soaked and cooked before eating), 2) the FDA can require that a label reveal facts that are material in light of (i.e., necessary to correct or balance) other representations made by the manufacturer or seller on behalf of the food. Accordingly, in the 1992 announcement, the FDA said that labeling is required "if a food derived from a new plant variety differs from its traditional counterpart such that the common or usual name no longer applies to the new food, or if a safety or usage issue exists to which consumers must be alerted." The policy statement also emphasized that, as for other foods derived from new plant varieties, no premarket review or approval is required unless the characteristics of the biotech food explicitly raise safety issues; and that, inasmuch as the genetic method used in the development of a new plant variety does not meet either of the two criteria above for "materiality," the agency cannot require that labeling include this information.

The 1992 policy has already been tested in a way that constitutes a kind of experimental "positive control." [American biotech company] Pioneer Hi-Bred International produced a recombinant soybean for the improvement of the quality of animal feed that also manifested allergenicity common to Brazil nut proteins. However, before release of the product, in the course of consultation and analysis required under the FDA policy, Pioneer Hi-Bred International identified the allergenicity. Confronted with the dual prospects of potential product liability and the costs of labeling all products derived from the new plant variety, the company abandoned all plans for using the new soybeans in consumer products. Not a single consumer was exposed to injury by the soybeans.

The FDA's approach to food labeling has been consistent with the scientific consensus that the risks associated with recombinant organisms and the products derived from them are fundamentally the same as those for other products. Dozens of new plant varieties modified with traditional genetic techniques (such as hybridization and mutagenesis) enter the marketplace every year without premarket regulatory review or special labeling. Many of these products are from "wide crosses," in which genes have been moved across natural breeding barriers, that is, from one species or genus to another (but without the use of recombinant DNA techniques). None of these plants exists in nature. None is required to have or in fact receives a premarket review by a government agency. (Safety tests by plant breeders consist primarily of assessment of taste and appearance and, in the case of plants with high levels of known intrinsic toxicants such as tomato and potato, measurement of the levels of certain alkaloids.) Nonetheless, they have become an integral, familiar, and safe part of our diet: they include bread and durum wheat, corn, rice, oats, black currants, pumpkins, tomatoes, and potatoes.

One aspect of the significance of moving genes across large taxonomic distances has been addressed by the massive accumulation in recent years of sequencing data, which show extensive genetic homology between the genomes of organisms that are only remotely related. For example, the sequencing of the *Escherichia coli* genome reveals that its DNA sequences share identity with organisms as distantly related as canola, amphibians, birds, grasses and mammals, including humans. These and other similar findings from genomic sequencing put in doubt the value of unequivocally assigning to a species the "proprietorship," or "normal location," of a gene.

The Costs of Labeling

Certain special-interest groups have called for stringent labeling requirements, but such regulations and labeling requirements are not in the best interest of consumers. As food producers know well, a requirement for various kinds of information on a label can add significantly to the production costs of certain foods, particularly those that are produced from pooled fresh fruits and vegetables. To maintain the accuracy of labels, recombinant DNA-modified fruits and vegetables would have to be segregated through all phases of production—planting, harvesting, processing, and distribution—which adds costs and compromises economies of scale. These added production costs constitute, in effect, a special tax levied on those producers who choose to use a new, superior technology. These added costs are a particular disadvantage to new products in the highly competitive, low-profit-margin marketplace of processed foods, and their impacts are felt throughout the production pipeline. They reduce profits to plant breeders, farmers, food processors, grocers, and others in the distribution pathway; decrease competition; and increase prices to consumers.

Furthermore, overregulation, in the form of compulsory labeling, can change the course of future research and development. Within the United States and internationally, under various current regulatory regimes for field testing that focus exclusively on organisms manipulated with recombinant DNA techniques, research and development have become limited primarily to a small number of commodity crops that are grown on a vast scale, at the expense of opportunities to improve important small-acreage crops. In 1999, worldwide, the top four recombinant crops (soybean, corn, cotton, and canola or rapeseed oil) accounted for more than 99% of the global acreage; currently, innovation seldom targets the improvement of the genetics of environmentally threatened but low-value-added species such as trees or of subsistence crops such as millet, cassava, and yams.

Fortunately, unscientific and anti-innovative regulatory policies toward biotech foods in the United States are likely to remain in the realm of speculation. The language of the FDA's principal enabling statute (the Federal Food, Drug and Cosmetic Act) firmly supports—indeed, to a large extent, dictates—the FDA's science-based and commonsense policies toward biotech foods. And these policies were upheld indirectly by the U.S. Court of Appeals for the Second Circuit, which found in a pivotal 1996 decision regarding another product of biotechnology that food labeling cannot be compelled just because some consumers wish to have the information. In overturning a Vermont law that required labeling of dairy products from cows treated with recombination bovine somatotropin (a polypeptide hormone that increases the productivity of dairy cows), the court found that such regulation merely to satisfy the public's "right to know" is a constitutional violation of commercial free speech. "Were consumer interest alone sufficient, there is no end to the information that states could require manufacturers to disclose about their production methods," the court wrote, in *International Dairy Foods Association v. Amestoy.*

Finally, there is the critical but largely unaddressed question of the economics of required labeling. A 1994 analysis of the economic impacts of a labeling requirement for new biotech foods by the California Department of Consumer Affairs, a state watchdog agency, predicted that the additional costs would be "substantial" and that "while the American food processing industry is large, it is doubtful that it would be either willing or able to absorb most of the additional costs associated with labeling biotech foods." The analysis concluded that "there is cause for concern that consumers will be unwilling to pay even the increased price for biotech foods necessary to cover biotechnology research and development, much less the additional price increases necessary to cover the costs associated with labeling biotech food."

The California Department of Consumer Affairs' assessment implies another outcome of unwarranted but compulsory labeling. Overregulation, in the form of required labeling, would increase costs, reduce competition, and thus increase prices; and the availability of overpriced biotech products would be skewed toward upscale, higher-income markets. Wealthier consumers would be able to pay more for the improved products; the less affluent would simply do without them. (This phenomenon has already occurred on an international scale: with field trials of recombinant DNA-modified plants grossly overregulated around the world and the costs of performing them inflated relative to similar non-recombinant plants, there is little impetus to use molecular techniques to develop improved varieties of plants common in subsistence agriculture, such as millet, cassava, and yams.)

The Psychology of Labeling

Inasmuch as there appears to be little flexibility for U.S. regulators to require regressive, unnecessary and costly labeling, why is so much attention paid to the issue? The answer lies in the intentions and actions of the ideological opponents of the new biotechnology, who have for decades used a variety of strategies to inhibit research and development and commerce. Unsuccessful at attempting to elicit consumer skepticism and at petitioning and suing government agencies to enjoin them from approving the testing and marketing of new biotech products, these activists have sought regulations that would require labeling to reveal the use of molecular techniques of genetic manipulation. Labeling raises costs, which discourages producers and consumers, and destroys markets for new products, so for those wishing to block the commercialization of biotech products, forcing an increase in costs by means of unnecessary labeling is an effective strategy. Regulatory stringency is also an unmistakable signal to the public, implying that there is something fundamentally different and worrisome about biotech foods. Antibiotechnology activists argue that we need regulation because consumers are apprehensive, and, then, when consumers become apprehensive *because* the products are stringently regulated, the activists say we need more regulation to assuage consumers' concerns. The objective is to replicate activists' success in getting consumers to reject irradiated foods in the 1980s. At that time, federal regulators responded to a prolonged campaign by requiring that irradiated foods be specially labeled with a logo that could only be interpreted as a consumer warning. Activists opposed to the new technology were then able to convince consumers that the foods were altered in ways that compromised safety. The psychological aspect of this strategy is conveyed by the observations of Barbara Keating-Edh, representing the consumer-advocacy group *Consumer Alert* before the National Biotechnology Policy Board, September 20, 1991: "For obvious reasons, the consumer views the technologies that are *most* regulated to be the *least* safe ones. Heavy involvement by government, no matter how well intended, inevitably sends the wrong signals. Rather than ensuring confidence, it raises suspicion and doubt."

The FDA's current policy toward labeling biotech food is in stark contrast to that in Europe and Asia, where regulators have shown a willingness to permit politics, public misapprehensions, the blandishments of antitechnology activists, and nescience to dictate regulatory policy. The European Union, for example, introduced mandatory labeling of gene-spliced foods [in 1998], which Britain's agriculture minister called "a triumph for consumer rights to better information," and which a senior regulator characterized as "a question of choice, of consumer choice." But because of the labeling law, there is hardly any choice now at all. Britain's new law sparked a stampede by manufacturers, retailers, and restaurant chains to rid their products of all genetically modified ingredients so they would not have to introduce new "warning" labels and risk losing sales.

The existing FDA policy toward gene-spliced and other

novel foods has worked admirably. It involves the government only in those extraordinarily rare instances when products raise safety issues, and products are labeled only when consumers need to be warned about factors related to safety or to new patterns of usage. In all other instances, market forces are permitted to work their magic, the result of which has been unprecedented choice for farmers, food producers, and consumers and the unquestioned preeminence of American companies in the development and marketing of biotech foods.

Problems with Patenting Genes: The Case of *Monsanto v. Schmeiser*

TERRY J. ZAKRESKI

In 1997 Canadian canola farmer Percy Schmeiser was routinely spraying herbicide along a ditch when he discovered that some of his canola plants had become herbicide-resistant, a sign that they were contaminated by pollen from Monsanto's patented herbicide-resistant canola. Monsanto's canola, known as Roundup Ready, is genetically engineered to be resistant to Monsanto's Roundup herbicide. Planting the special canola allows farmers to spray weeds without harming the canola crop. In August 1998 Monsanto filed a lawsuit against Schmeiser for patent infringement, alleging that the farmer had infringed the company's patent by growing Roundup Ready canola and harvesting the seeds without a license. Schmeiser countered that he was not responsible for the seeds being introduced to his land, suggesting that they might have blown off a passing seed truck or from neighboring farms. The farmer also noted that because his 1998 crop was a mix of his own strain and Monsanto's, there was no advantage to be gained from the presence of the Roundup Ready strain as he could not use Roundup on the crop without killing off his own canola.

Terry J. Zakreski, trial brief on behalf of the defendants Percy Schmeiser and Schmeiser Enterprises Ltd., *Monsanto v. Schmeiser*, Canada, June 2002.

In the following excerpt from the 2002 trial brief, Terry J. Zakreski, Schmeiser's lawyer, argues that Schmeiser did nothing wrong and should not be required to pay Monsanto damages. Zakreski criticizes the company for not making an effort to prevent its special canola from contaminating other canola plants. Controversially, the court ruled in favor of Monsanto, setting what Monsanto called "a world standard in intellectual property protection."

Percy Schmeiser is 69 years of age. He has been growing canola since the early 1950s. He follows his own practices for the growing of canola, including saving and reusing his own canola seed from crop year to crop year. This is not an unusual farming practice and has been a fundamental right enjoyed by farmers in Canada. Even though Mr. Schmeiser did nothing but follow his usual practice of saving and reusing his own canola seed in 1997 and 1998, he and Schmeiser Enterprises Ltd., the corporation through which he carries on his farming operation, now find themselves being prosecuted by a large multinational company alleging that in 1998 they infringed its patent.

The Plaintiffs, Monsanto Canada Inc. and Monsanto Company (referred to hereafter as "Monsanto"), have alleged that Mr. Schmeiser deliberately grew a Roundup resistant canola crop in 1998 from seed that he saved from his 1997 canola crop, which Monsanto alleges infringes its patent.

There do appear to be Roundup resistant canola plants growing on Mr. Schmeiser's property against his wishes. This is the result of contamination of Mr. Schmeiser's seed supply, and not by design. Monsanto cannot control, and has never tried to control, the spread of its gene around the countryside. They have contaminated Mr. Schmeiser's fields and now they are suing him for patent infringement.

The Farming Practices of Percy Schmeiser

Mr. Schmeiser has been growing canola since the 1950s. Ken Kirkland, an expert tendered by the Plaintiffs, admitted that such experience would make Mr. Schmeiser an experienced canola grower. After growing canola over many years, Mr. Schmeiser has developed his own farming practices particular to the land that he farms, which practices have withstood experimentation and the test of time.

Percy Schmeiser's canola crops have performed much better than average in bushels per acre. His canola crops are relatively free of common diseases that plague canola, such as black-leg, and are also relatively free of weeds.

Mr. Schmeiser has not put in one crop insurance claim for any of his canola crops due to farming methods, and in fact, he receives a premium discount on his canola crop insurance due to his claims experience.

Mr. Schmeiser saves and reuses his own canola seed. Many other farmers choose to do so. Farmers still have the right to choose and Mr. Schmeiser chose, at all relevant times, to save and reuse his own seed rather than being reliant on seed companies, or incurring what he sees to be an unnecessary expense. The last time that Mr. Schmeiser bought canola seed was in 1993, before the crop year of 1999 when he was forced to buy canola seed to fight the contamination of his crops by the Roundup resistant volunteer canola. . . .

A Successful Canola Farmer

Mr. Schmeiser does use herbicides for weed control. He will incorporate herbicide in the spring (or in the fall where he is dealing with a summer-fallow field or a field in which he is not growing canola back-to-back). Herbicides used for such purposes include Treflan (Rival). Since the herbicide is incorporated in the soil, it controls weeds before they grow. According to Mr. Schmeiser such soil incorporation of herbicide will last up to three years.

In the spring, as is common farming practice, Mr. Schmeiser will burn off fields with Roundup herbicide before planting (a "spring burn-off"). He will also use Roundup herbicide to "chem fallow" fields [control weeds]. Both

Mr. Kirkland and Mr. [Aaron] Mitchell [Monsanto's biotechnology manager] agreed that this is a common and acceptable use of Roundup by a conventional canola grower. After the crop is in and growing, Mr. Schmeiser uses other herbicides such as Muster and Assure which are safe to spray on canola to control weeds on an as-needed basis. Mr. Schmeiser does not, and did not, spray Roundup on his growing canola, as this would be disastrous to the canola crop. After the crop is in and growing Roundup does have a use, in spraying for weeds and volunteers around power poles and in the ditches, and for chem fallow.

All in all, Mr. Schmeiser's farming practices have proved to be effective. His canola seed, and the crops grown from it, are a source of great personal pride and accomplishment. He is, by all standards, a successful canola farmer.

The Nature of Monsanto's Invention

Monsanto is not a seed company. Monsanto sells no canola seeds in Canada. It has proprietary know-how that allows it to take a gene from other organisms and introduce it into plants such as canola. Once introduced, the extra gene gives the plant glyphosate resistance. This gene, and the insertion thereof into certain plants, is now the subject of a patent held by the Defendant Monsanto Company.

The Defendant, Monsanto Company, obtained Patent No. 1-313-80830 (the "Invention") on February 23, 1993. Monsanto Company licenses Monsanto Canada Inc. to use the Invention in Canada. Regulatory approval was obtained in 1995 for the unconfined release into the environment of the gene mentioned in the Invention. Commercial sales of the canola seed began in 1996. Monsanto delivers seeds containing the gene to seed companies who cross-breed the seed with their own canola plants and sell their canola seeds to farmers.

A canola plant containing the gene mentioned in the Invention behaves no differently than any other canola plant. Canola plants, whether conventional or genetically-altered, produce seeds. Wherever the genetically-modified canola seed is spread, whether by wind, blown off trucks, carried with water during spring runoff, or from farm implements, new genetically-modified canola will grow. Generally, farmers describe canola that has spread and is growing where it was not deliberately planted as "volunteer" canola.

The genetically-modified canola also produces genetically-modified pollen. Canola is an open-pollinated crop. This means that pollen from genetically-modified canola plants will fertilize other conventional canola plants, and their progeny will carry the Roundup resistant characteristic. The gene introduced into the genetically-modified canola expresses itself as a dominant gene. By the application of basic genetics, if a canola plant with the herbicide-tolerant characteristic fertilizes a Roundup susceptible canola plant all the progeny from that canola plant will be resistant to Roundup.

By seeds or by pollen, Monsanto's invention can spread to places it was not planted or intended to be grown. The spread of seeds, whether by farming practices or by natural means, and the flow of pollen imparts to Monsanto's invention a unique characteristic not seen with any other "invention" protected under the Patent Act. The Invention has the unique ability to replicate itself and invade land and plants where it was not intended. Monsanto has not, and never attempted to, control the spread of its gene around the countryside. . . .

Origin of the Roundup Resistant Seed

It has never been disputed that the Defendants' 1997 crop contained Roundup resistant canola. This canola was located on Field #2, on an area of approximately 3 acres. This canola seed, because it was used to plant the Defendants' 1998 crop, caused the contamination of that year's crop. The issue which must be determined is where the Roundup resistant canola seen in 1997 originated.

It is clear this canola seed was not deliberately planted

by Mr. Schmeiser. He has steadfastly and consistently denied doing so. One very important fact is the distribution of the surviving canola. It was thickest near the road, and thinned moving into the field. [Plant breeder] Dr. [Keith] Downey agreed that if an air seeder was used, and Roundup Ready canola was mixed in, a random distribution would be expected.

The Plaintiffs contend that the seed which contaminated the 1997 crop could not have come off passing trucks, because the 1996 herbicide-tolerant canola crop was identity preserved. The Identity Preservation Program was dropped in 1997 and, beginning in 1997, farmers could transport and sell the canola like any other canola grown in Saskatchewan. It must be remembered that the purpose of the Identity Preservation Program was to ensure that the herbicide-tolerant canola was sold to the right elevator. The program was never intended to stem the spread of genetically-modified canola around the countryside by seed dispersal and pollen contamination. Farmers were not required to tarp their canola during transport from the field to grain bins so that seed would not blow off their grain trucks. They were not required to keep a buffer zone. They were not required to clean equipment. And they were not required to warn their neighbours about herbicide-tolerant volunteers. . . .

Evidence was also tendered to establish that swaths of canola can travel great distances in the wind. Indeed, Mr. Schmeiser's neighbour, Al Huber, grew Roundup Ready canola in 1996. Swaths from this field blew into Field #6, which swaths likely also contaminated his seed supply.

"One Hungry Bee"

The only scientific studies done about the spread of genetically-modified canola appear to have been done regarding pollen movement. Genetically-modified canola can pollinate non-genetically modified canola. Because the gene that gives plants Roundup resistance is a dominant gene, a Roundup-susceptible canola plant can be pollinated and all its progeny will be Roundup-tolerant. The recent contamination problem with canola which was supposed to be non-genetically modified that was shipped to Europe is proof in and of itself that pollen will travel much further than had been anticipated.

Furthermore, Dr. Downey's opinions regarding pollen contamination are predicated on an assumed fact as to where Roundup Ready canola was grown in each of the years 1996, 1997 and 1998. This opinion is only as good as the evidence on which it is based, which only consists of Monsanto's information. For example, farmers could have grown it on land descriptions other than what is stated in their license, and canola growers could have grown it without a license. Because genetically-modified canola looks the same as conventional canola, there is no way for a farmer to know which field the canola may be growing on.

Additionally, it must be remembered that, in the words of Dr. Downey, "one hungry bee" can travel a considerable distance. Cross pollination occurs, and likely to a greater extent than was anticipated.

As to what exactly caused the contamination of Field #2 in 1997, who is able to say without speculating? All that matters is how the Plaintiffs' gene *did not* get on his land: It did not get there as a result of Mr. Schmeiser obtaining bootlegged seed and deliberately planting it. This allegation was dropped by the Plaintiffs. It could have arrived in a variety of ways—off a truck, broken seed bags, wind blown swaths or pollen from Mr. Huber's land to Field #6, spring run off, and passing equipment.

No Utility to Grow a Mixed Crop

All witnesses agreed that there in no utility in growing a mixed Roundup Ready/Roundup susceptible crop. The advantage in growing Roundup Ready canola is that a grower may spray in-crop with Roundup and achieve broad spectrum weed control. If a grower plants a crop which is a mixture of Roundup Ready and Roundup susceptible canola, he cannot spray in-crop with Roundup. To do so would be suicide.

Accordingly, it defies logic that the Defendants would have saved the seed from the "test strip", which included Roundup resistant and Roundup susceptible canola, mixed that seed with bin-run conventional canola, all in some deliberate move to take advantage of the Plaintiffs' patent. During the course of this Trial, it was clear that Mr. Schmeiser is, and has always been, a conventional canola grower. He does not believe his farming practices can benefit from growing a herbicide-tolerant crop. He took great pride in the seed he had developed over the course of some 40 years. In particular, growing Roundup Ready canola would not allow him to continue his practice of growing canola back to back.

The evidence confirmed that Mr. Schmeiser continued to use Treflan (Rival), Muster, and Assure to achieve weed control. . . . He would not have done so if he was growing a Roundup Ready crop. His Roundup use is consistent with a conventional canola grower. Furthermore, the University of Manitoba test results prove he did not in-crop spray with Roundup in the opinion of [professor of plant science] Dr. [René] Van Aker.

The Defendants would not, and did not, plant a Roundup Ready crop. . . .

Monsanto's Patent

Monsanto does not own a patent for a canola plant. It owns a patent for a gene. This gene comes from other organisms and is added to a plant such as a canola plant to give it glyphosate resistance. It is something added to the gene structure of the plant. It neither causes the plant to grow, nor causes it to grow any better. It is merely something superfluous to the plant unless it happens to be challenged by glyphosate-based herbicide.

To grow canola is not to use the gene. This is because

the gene does not cause canola to grow. The invention has no utility unless a farmer is spraying his canola with Roundup intending it to survive. Only then is he using the gene technology patented by Monsanto. There is no utility, and no use of the gene technology, if the farmer grows a mixed crop.

The rights given to a patent holder under the *Patent Act* are contained in Section 42 of the Act. Those rights include ". . . the exclusive right, privilege and liberty of making, constructing and using the invention and selling it to others to be used. . . ."

It is to be noted that the list does not include the exclusive right to "possess" an invention. In other words, it is not patent infringement to merely possess an invention, only to use it. . . .

Contamination of the Environment

Roundup Ready canola could not be contained the minute it was introduced into the rural environment in Saskatchewan and commercially sold. It was Monsanto's obligation to control its own technology to ensure that it did not spread about. They have not attempted to do so. They cannot put the obligation on the farmer to keep this gene out of his property.

This issue becomes particularly problematical if Monsanto continues to bring actions for patent infringement merely from a farmer having canola plants with their gene growing on his land. If this is the case, Monsanto should simply be allowed to collect royalties from every seeded acre of canola growing in western Canada, and particularly, in the Rural Municipality of Bayne, because there is no way of ensuring that their canola gene has not spread to, or soon will have spread to, every seeded acre of canola growing in the Rural Municipality of Bayne.

The evidence showed that 40% of the seeded acres of canola in western Canada are seeded with Roundup Ready canola. Mr. Schmeiser, in his testimony and through the numerous photographs he has taken, has painstakingly documented the contamination of the Rural Municipality of Bayne by the Monsanto gene since 1998. His photographs of surviving canola plants where he has sprayed Roundup in many different locations in the town of Bruno and on his fields nearby establishes the extent of the contamination of the environment. And if canola plants have Roundup resistance it can be safely concluded that it was caused by Monsanto's gene. . . .

Schmeiser Did Not Profit

The Plaintiffs have made it abundantly clear that they are seeking to make a public example of Percy Schmeiser.

The Plaintiffs have named Mr. Schmeiser as a defendant in this action, notwithstanding the overwhelming evidence that all the farming activities in question were conducted through Schmeiser's Enterprises Ltd. The cases cited by the Plaintiffs do not support piercing the corporate veil. Mr. Schmeiser did nothing that would not be within the ordinary course of business for his company. He farmed. They are clearly after him personally.

Furthermore, they have persisted in suggesting that Mr. Schmeiser committed a quasi-fraudulent act without any proof, and even after having withdrawn this allegation from their claim. They have not shied away from calling him a liar and a person without any credibility.

Monsanto also seeks the profits from the Defendants' 1998 canola crop, not the $15 per acre license fee. This, notwithstanding the fact that it was their gene that invaded the Defendants' crops. They claim this invasion entitles them to the ownership of the profits from the 1998 crop.

The Defendants did not make a penny more because Monsanto's gene contaminated their seed supply. The canola seed was sold at the same price as conventional canola. The Defendants sold their canola to a crushing plant, not to another farmer to be used. If they did not in-crop spray with Roundup, they received no benefit from the Plaintiffs' gene being in their fields. The Defendants did not and could not have profited from it. Nonetheless, the Plaintiffs are claiming the entire profit the Defendants made from the sale of *their* canola in 1998 merely because the Monsanto gene attached itself to the Defendants' property. Their gene invaded the Defendants' seed supply, and now they must turn over their canola to Monsanto because the gene cannot be returned. The Plaintiffs do not even wish to compensate Mr. Schmeiser for the labour he put into growing this crop.

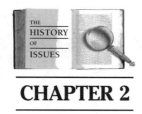

CHAPTER 2

Engineered Animals

Chapter Preface

On April 12, 1988, the U.S. Patent and Trademark Office (PTO) issued a patent for a transgenic animal called Oncomouse. The mouse, engineered to be susceptible to tumors and named after the cancer-causing oncogene, was the first animal to be given patent protection. Researchers and corporations could now claim intellectual property rights over any living organism and the technologies used to create them.

The patent has created intense controversy. Some researchers complain that patent law is hampering their work. For example, American firm DuPont, which funded the original research on Oncomouse, currently holds the patent on the creature and therefore lays broad claims to medical discoveries made with its product. Many researchers argue that such broad patents reduce future research investment by institutions concerned about violating patented intellectual property rights. On the other hand, life patent proponents argue that the economic benefits of patent protection will encourage scientific research. If a company can be assured that it will be granted a life patent, it will be more likely to invest in research. In proponents' view patents offset the financial risks associated with pursuing cutting-edge scientific research, which often requires large initial investments.

The Oncomouse controversy also provoked a more general debate about the morality of exploiting animals. While it is true that humans have utilized animals for both food and labor for thousands of years, many critics contend that the manipulation of animals' genetic code goes too far. These opponents argue that through the combination of genetic engineering and life patenting, animals had become simply a means to an end. Engineering animals to be susceptible to cancer is also cruel, they point out. Supporters of the Oncomouse maintain that the potential for a cancer cure significantly outweighs concerns about the well-being of mice. They also note that genetically modifying animals may one day lead to cures of other diseases besides cancer, new drugs, and cheaper food.

The creation of the Oncomouse has entered the long-standing debate over animal rights, but it has also ignited a new controversy over life patents. While the Oncomouse could lead to a cure for cancer, it could also wind up hampering research and diminish humanity's relationship with animals. As scientists continue to modify animals for use in laboratories and on farms, the debate is sure to intensify.

Milk from Genetically Engineered Cows Is Harmful

GRETA GAARD

In November 1993 the U.S. Food and Drug Administration approved biotech firm Monsanto's product Posilac, making milk the first food produced using genetic engineering. Posilac, or recombinant bovine growth hormone (rBGH), is a manufactured hormone that, when injected into lactating cows, increases milk yields by 10 to 15 percent. It is produced by taking the naturally occurring growth hormone gene from cows, modifying it slightly, and inserting it into bacteria. The modified hormone is only slightly different from the natural version, with just one amino acid substituted for another at the end of a large molecule. Nonetheless, a controversy over the hormone ensued, with proponents arguing that increased milk production could help alleviate world hunger, and opponents contending that the hormone made the milk unsafe to drink.

In the following selection from 1994 Greta Gaard, renowned activist and scholar in the fields of ecofeminism and Green politics, argues that although the results of scientific research are inconclusive, there is evidence to suggest that rBGH-produced milk is harmful to humans and that rBGH definitely harms the injected animals. Furthermore, she argues that despite the claims of rBGH proponents, the use of rBGH is un-

necessary, as increased milk production will neither help alleviate world hunger nor benefit dairy farmers.

M ilk is the first genetically engineered food to be sold in the United States. On 5 November 1993, the US Food and Drug Administration (FDA) approved recombinant Bovine Growth Hormone (rBGH)—known in Britain as recombinant Bovine Somatotropin (BST)—for use in dairy cattle. Bovine Growth Hormone is a natural protein made by cows; rBGH, however, is a genetically engineered, synthetic version, developed and tested in laboratories and in field trials over the past 10 years by drug and chemical companies such as Monsanto, Upjohn, Eli Lilley and American Cyanamid. Injected every 14 days into dairy cows for 200 days of a cow's 335-day lactation cycle, it increases milk production dramatically.

Supporters of rBGH argue that the hormone is a naturally occurring substance; people need milk; extra milk is needed to feed the poor in the United States and in Third World countries; and increased milk production will make farmers that more competitive. None of these claims provide a valid reason for using rBGH. Starting from its injection into the cows all the way through to the production and consumption of rBGH milk, and dairy and meat products, the genetically engineered hormone has a deleterious effect on the health and well-being of humans, animals and the earth. The only entities which stand to benefit from rBGH are the industrial and governmental bureaucracies which promote it.

Bovine Machines

In the current industrial system of factory farming, cows are production machines. Kept in a perpetual cycle of gestation and lactation, their bodies wear out quickly; a cow's life span is cut from 20 to 25 years down to five years or less. Her calves are taken away from her, often only 24 hours after birth. Some are confined in small wooden crates for their short lives of 15 weeks, during which they are fed an iron-deficient diet to obtain white rather than dark meat. When they reach the optimum weight of 330 pounds, they are slaughtered for veal. All the while, the cow's milk flows to feed humans.

Cows already overproduce milk. In 1930, the average cow in the US produced 12 pounds of milk per day; in 1988, milk production was at 39 pounds per day; with rBGH injections, it is expected to reach 49 pounds per day, four times more than "natural". Because rBGH-injected cows cannot consume and digest enough grass for hyperlactation, they have to be fed a highly concentrated diet and are not allowed to graze. More vulnerable to disease, they receive more doses of antibiotics. For instance, mastitis, a bacterial infection leading to painful inflammation of the udder, increases with the use of rBGH, and both pus and antibiotic residues can pass into the milk. Cows injected with rBGH also have an increased incidence of foot and leg ailments, persistent body sores and lacerations, digestive disorders and higher body temperatures. Many farmers are already suspicious of the fact that Monsanto gives a veterinary service voucher of over $100 with every initial order of Posilac, its brand name for rBGH.

Minnesota dairy farmer John Kurtz, who participated in a three-and-a-half-year study on the effects of rBGH, commented that although milk production increased 18 per cent during the first lactation of cows injected with rBGH, none of the cows stayed in the herd after the second lactation because none of them conceived and 24 per cent died. rBGH-injected cows are also at greater risk of developing Bovine Spongiform Encephalopathy (BSE), commonly known as "mad cow disease", since the energy-dense food that rBGH-injected cows require often contains BSE-infected meat and bone meal.

Implications for Human Health

Although both Monsanto and the US FDA claim that laboratory tests cannot find traces of rBGH in milk products, and no effects of rBGH's impact on cows can be transmitted to humans, many questions still remain. Cows injected with rBGH produce much more IGF-1, an insulin-like growth factor. The molecular structure of IGF-1 is the same in humans as in cows, increasing the likelihood of its transmission through cow milk and meat consumption. In humans, IGF-1 causes acromegaly, a disease characterized by the abnormal enlargement of the hands, feet, nose and chin. Increased levels of IGF-1 have also been linked to colon tumours and cancer, particularly breast cancer in women. According to Dr Samuel Epstein, Professor of Occupational and Environmental Medicine at the University of Illinois-Chicago, "IGF-1 is a growth factor for human breast cells, maintaining their malignancy, progression, and invasiveness." Transmission of IGF-1 from cows to humans is made even more likely by the fact that 40 per cent of the beef used to make hamburgers comes from "spent" dairy cows.

In February 1994, fast-food multinationals McDonalds and Pizza Hut announced that they would use rBGH-produced milk and meat products. This will have particular impact on the poor and working classes who do not have the economic "freedom" to "choose" organic foods—and thus on a disproportionate number of women, women-headed households, people of colour and children. People of every class and race frequent fast-food chains; but such outlets are often the only restaurants in small or rural communities, while in urban centres, they provide quick meals to single-parent and working families.

Several school lunch programmes have chosen to boycott rBGH milk products, because growing children are more vulnerable to hormones and chemicals than adults. An early onset of puberty is thought to be caused by the increased general use of hormones in Western societies, and girls who menstruate before the age of 12 are at a higher risk of contracting breast cancer later in life.

Advocates of rBGH claim that higher milk output will increase the amount of food available worldwide. The genetically engineered hormone has already been licensed for sale in Brazil, Mexico and South Africa, while field trials are again underway in Argentina, China, Egypt, India, Malaysia, Pakistan, Tunisia, Zambia and Zimbabwe. But introducing rBGH in these countries and advocating increases in milk production may supplant cheaper, more traditional sources of food.

Many people worldwide cannot, in fact, digest cows' milk because of lactose intolerance. Moreover, the steady aggregate surplus of milk and butter for the past decade has not increased its availability to the poor. Such facts indicate that physical scarcity of milk is not a factor in world hunger.

The use of rBGH may even increase such hunger and the structures supporting it. Excessive animal consumption, as is predominant in many Western diets, is already a "protein factory in reverse." A single acre can feed 20 times as many people eating a vegetarian diet than it can feed people eating an animal-based diet. In the US, animals are fed over 80 per cent of the corn grown in the country, and over 95 per cent of the oats. This practice of feeding livestock rather than people means that less food is available for people. Already many developing countries are growing cash crops, rather than subsistence crops, leading to shortages of domestic food.

Loss of Small Farmers

It is estimated that dairy farm income in the US will drop $1.3 billion [from 1994 to 2000] because of the use of rBGH. By the turn of the century, annual losses due to the growth hormone will climb to $546 million. Up to 30 per cent of dairy farmers may be forced out of business within three years of its legalization, a loss which will be felt not only by dairy farmers, but by entire rural communities. For each dairy farmer who goes out of business, 25 dairy-related jobs are lost.

rBGH drives small farmers out of business because of the cost of buying the hormone, the higher cost of specialized feed, and the cost of "burning out" the cows. Whereas agribusinesses, whose herds often number between 5,000 and 10,000 cows, can afford to purchase "high energy" feed in bulk, small farmers cannot. Moreover, a three per cent surplus in milk production can mean a 30 per cent decrease in the price the farmer gets, since US farmers who produce more than they did the previous year are taxed extra for overproduction.

Farmers who reject rBGH, however, are depicted by the "experts" as less sophisticated and "behind the times". Ironically, their reluctance to "adapt to technology" is seen as hastening the bankruptcy of small family farms, and the domination of large-scale, corporate agribusiness.

Consumers Reject rBGH

An increase in milk production will not reduce costs for the consumer. The US government already spends $1 billion annually to purchase surplus milk supplies in the form of butter. The milk support programme is estimated to have risen by at least $65 million in 1994 alone, and is set to increase another $116 million in fiscal year 1995. Taxpayers will pay these costs, while the drug companies profit. Moreover, 11 consumer surveys show that consumers do not want to buy milk produced with rBGH.

Opinion poll research has also revealed that consumers would not purchase products developed with a "growth hormone". Accordingly, chemical companies and research laboratories prefer to call rBGH Somatotropin or, when pressured, Bovine Somatotropin. The manufacturers' refusal to name their product for what it is, is illustrated in their battle against labelling. Consumer groups, worried about the possible human health effects of rBGH, have repeatedly requested labelling of dairy products that are rBGH-free, rBGH advocates claim that labelling will "have the inherent effect of causing consumers to believe that such [rBGH] products are different from and inferior to milk products from unsupplemented cows."

The Commodification of Animals

ANDREW KIMBRELL

On April 12, 1988, the U.S. Patent and Trademark Office issued the first patent on a living animal for the "Harvard Mouse." The mouse was a genetically engineered animal predisposed to develop cancer, allowing researchers to better understand carcinogens. Since that decision, hundreds of applications have been submitted for the patenting of transgenic animals, engineered to provide superior research specimens or to improve food production. In the rush to claim potentially lucrative patents, researchers have produced a wide variety of modified animals, many of which have displayed unexpected and grotesque deformities.

In the following selection from 1996 Andrew Kimbrell, a public interest attorney and executive director of the Center for Food Safety, writes that despite such setbacks and against the wishes of the public, the engineering and patenting of animals continue unabated. Kimbrell argues that what is needed is a "biodemocracy" that would restrict genetic engineering and ban the patenting of life, forcing researchers and corporations to conform to public opinion. To date, no such moratorium has occurred.

B iotechnology extends humanity's reach over the forces of nature as no technology in history has ever done.

Bioengineers are now manipulating life forms in much the same way as the engineers of the Industrial Revolution were able to separate, collect, utilize, and exploit inanimate materials. Just as previous generations manipulated plastics and metals into the machines and products of the Industrial Age, we are now manipulating and indeed transferring living materials into the new commodities of the global age of biotechnology.

The Manipulation of Life Forms

With current technology, it is becoming possible to snip, insert, recombine, edit, and program genetic material, the very blueprint of life. Using these techniques, the new life-engineers are rearranging the genetic structures of the living world, crossing and intermixing species at will to create thousands of novel microbes, plants, and animals. Recent examples include pigs engineered with human growth genes to increase their size; tomatoes engineered with flounder genes to resist cold temperatures; salmon with cattle growth genes spliced in to increase their size; tobacco plants engineered with the fluorescent gene of fireflies to make them glow at night; and laboratory mice encoded with the AIDS virus as part of their permanent genetic makeup.

Biotechnologists are also able to screen for and isolate valuable genetic material from virtually any living organism. They then can clone industrial amounts of valuable DNA, hormones, enzymes, and other biochemicals. Recent advances even allow the cloning of innumerable "xerox" copies of whole organisms, including higher mammals.

With these new capabilities, genetic engineering represents the ultimate tool in the manipulation of life forms. For the first time, scientists have the potential of becoming the architects of life itself, the initiators of an ersatz technological evolution designed to create new species of microbes, plants, and animals that are more profitable to enterprises involved in agriculture, industry, biomass energy production, and research.

The World's Genetic Resources

The raw material for this new enterprise is genetic resources. Just as the powers of the Industrial Age colonized the world in search of minerals and fossil fuels, the biocolonizers are now in search of new biological materials that can be transformed into profitable products through genetic engineering.

The new bio-prospectors know where to find the biodiversity they need. According to the World Resources Institute, more than half the world's plant and animal species live in the rain forests of the Third World—*and nowhere else on Earth.* The nonindustrialized world's coastal regions add millions more species to those already available to the new engineers of life. The Third World is now witnessing a "gene rush," as governments and multinational corporations aggressively scour forests and coasts in search of the new genetic gold. The human body is not immune from the reaches of the bio-prospectors. Organ and fetal transplantation, reproductive technology, and genetic manipulation of blood and cells have made body parts, including blood, organs, cells, and genes, extremely valuable. The collection and sale of human parts is becoming a major worldwide industry.

Many predict that the twenty-first century will become the age of biotechnology. Biocolonizing companies and governments know that the economic and political entities that control the genetic resources of the planet may well exercise decisive power over the world economy in coming decades. However, the new drive for international hegemony in the engineering and marketing of life represents an extraordinary threat to the earth's fragile ecosystems and to those living in them. Moreover, embarking on the long journey in which corporations and governments eventually become the brokers of the blueprints of life raises some of the most disturbing and important questions ever to face humanity: Do scientists and corporations have the right to alter the genetic code of life forms at will? Should we alter the genetic structure of the entire living kingdom in the name of utility or profit? Is there a limit to the number or type of human genes that should be allowed to be engineered into other animals? Should the genetic integrity of the biotic community be preserved? Is there something sacred about life, or should life forms, including the human body and its parts, be viewed simply as commodities in the new bio-tech marketplace? Is the genetic makeup of all living things the common heritage of all, or can it be appropriated by corporations and governments?

The companies, governments, and scientists at the forefront of the biorevolution—goaded by scientific curiosity or profit—have avoided virtually any discussion of the extraordinary implications of their actions. Further, the so-called "bioethicists" employed by various government and educational institutions appear incapable of saying no to any advance in the manipulation and sale of life. They seem intent on seeing the unthinkable become the debatable, the debatable become the justifiable, and the justifiable become the routine. While virtually all polls show that the international public is opposed to much of biotechnology and biocolonization, this has not yet led to a major biodemocracy movement that demands public participation and decision making in these issues. Without such a movement, the international biotechnology revolution, with all of its unprecedented environmental and ethical implications, will remain totally uncontrolled.

A Monopoly on Life Forms

The age of biocolonization was "officially" launched in 1980. That year witnessed a little-noted U.S. Supreme Court decision, *Diamond v. Chakrabarty*. This unheralded case will eventually be seen as one of the most important and infamous legal decisions of the century.

The case began in 1971, when Indian microbiologist Ananda Mohan Chakrabarty, an employee of General Electric (GE), developed a type of bacteria that could digest oil. GE quickly applied to the U.S. Patent and Trademark Office

(PTO) for a patent on Chakrabarty's genetically engineered oil-eating bacteria. After several years of review, the PTO rejected the GE patent application under the traditional legal doctrine that life forms ("products of nature") are not patentable.

Eventually, the case was appealed to the Supreme Court. GE and other corporations argued before the court that life forms were simply chemical products that could be patented just like any other "manufacture." A small number of public interest groups argued against the patenting of the microbe on the grounds that "to justify patenting living organisms, those who seek such patents must argue that life has no 'vital' or sacred property . . . and that once this is accomplished, all living material will be reduced to arrangements of chemicals, or 'mere compositions of matter.'" Opponents also reasoned that with patent profits as fuel, the accelerated drive to commercialize engineered life would eliminate all chance of objective public education and participation in the policy decisions involved.

Most expected the Supreme Court to support the PTO and to reject the GE patent. However, in June 1980, the Supreme Court handed down its surprise opinion. By a five-to-four margin, the court decided that Chakrabarty was to be granted his patent. *The highest court in the United States had decided that life was patentable.* The court dismissed the vision of a "parade of horribles" suggested by those who thought that the decision would lead to the engineering and patenting of higher life forms; it stated that the issue was not whether there was a "relevant distinction (in patentability) between living and inanimate things" but whether living products could be seen as "human-made inventions."

The next decade was to show that both patenting proponents and opponents were correct. Patenting did provide the economic trigger for a lucrative biotechnology industry, as GE had hoped. However, it also produced the "gruesome parade of horribles" feared by many and showed how inevitable was the slippery slope from the genetic engineering and patenting of microbes to that of plants, animals, and, finally, human genes, cells, and tissues.

The "Harvard Mouse"

Some called it the mouse that roared. Others called it the end of nature. On April 12, 1988, the PTO issued the first patent on a living animal (to Harvard Professor Philip Leder and Timothy A. Stewart of San Francisco) for their creation of a transgenic mouse containing a variety of genes derived from other species, including chickens and humans. The foreign genes were engineered into the mouse's permanent germline in order to predispose it to developing cancer, making it a better research animal on which to test the virulence of various carcinogens. While the media dubbed the patented animal the "Harvard mouse," it should really have been called the "DuPont mouse," since that company financed the Harvard research and now holds the license for its manufacture.

However, DuPont got a lot more than just a genetically engineered mouse from the PTO. The patent licensed to DuPont is extraordinarily broad, embracing any animals of any species, be they mice, rats, cats, or chimpanzees that are engineered to contain a variety of cancer-causing genes. The patent may well be among the broadest ever granted so far.

Eight other altered animal species, including mice, rabbits, and nematodes, have been patented. Currently, well over two hundred genetically engineered animals, including genetically manipulated fish, cows, sheep, and pigs, are standing in line to be patented by a variety of researchers and corporations.

Animals as Machines

The Patent and Trademark Office's decision to patent genetically altered animals was a direct result of the misguided *Chakrabarty* decision by the Supreme Court. In

1985, five years after the court's historic decision, the PTO ruled that *Chakrabarty* could be extended to apply to the patenting of genetically engineered plants, seeds, and plant tissue. Thus the entire plant kingdom was opened up to patent protection. Then on April 7, 1987, the PTO issued a ruling specifically extending the *Chakrabarty* decision to include all "multicellular living organisms, including animals." The radical new patenting policy suddenly transformed a Supreme Court decision on patenting microbes into one allowing the patenting of all life forms on Earth including animals. Under the ruling, a patented animal's legal status is no different from that of other manufactures such as automobiles or tennis balls.

It is doubtful that the PTO was prepared for the controversy it stirred up by issuing its edict permitting animal patenting. Editorials across the country lambasted the new policy. Bioethicist Robert Nelson saw it as "a staggering decision. . . . Once you start patenting life," he asked, "is there no stopping it?" . . .

As cells, genes, animals, and plants are now engineered and patented, most of the "gruesome parade of horribles" predicted by those opposing the 1980 *Chakrabarty* decision have become realities in dizzying rapidity.

"Perfect" Animals

Pig number 6707 was meant to be "super": super fast growing, super big, super meat quality. It was supposed to be a technological breakthrough in animal husbandry, among the first of a series of high-tech animals that would revolutionize agriculture and food production. Researchers at the United States Department of Agriculture (USDA) implanted the human gene governing growth into the pig while it was still an embryo. The idea was to have the human growth gene become part of the pig's genetic code and thus create an animal that, with the aid of the new gene, would grow far larger than any before.

To the surprise of the bioengineers, the human genetic

material that they had injected into the animal altered its metabolism in an unpredictable and unfortunate way. Transgenic pig number 6707 was in fact a tragicomic creation, a "super cripple." Excessively hairy, riddled with arthritis, and cross-eyed, the pig rarely even stood up, the wretched product of a science without ethics.

Despite such setbacks, researchers around the globe are creating thousands of transgenic creations like number 6707. They have inserted over two dozen different human genes into various fish, rodents, and mammals. Livestock containing human genes have become commonplace at research installations in the United States. Carp, catfish, and trout have been engineered with numbers of genes from humans, cattle, and rats to boost growth and reproduction. Researchers have used cell-fusion techniques to create *geeps*, astonishing sheep-goat combinations with the faces and horns of goats and the bodies of sheep. Chickens have been engineered so that they no longer contain the genetic trait for brooding, in order to make them more efficient egg producers.

Genetic engineers in the United States and Canada have also begun to successfully clone higher mammals. Although glitches have occurred, biotechnologists now feel they can alter animals to be more efficient sources of food and then clone unlimited copies of their patented "perfect" lamb, pig, or cow. . . .

The Commercial Reduction of Life

There are . . . potential human health problems [involved with genetically modifying food animals]. In May 1992, the U.S. Food and Drug Administration (FDA) approved the use of genetically engineered Bovine Growth Hormone (BGH) in cows to increase milk production. The animal drug produced by [American biotech company] Monsanto not only has devastating health impacts on dairy cows but also creates milk that has significantly higher levels of hormones and antibiotics. This milk is being sold, unlabeled, in countries around the globe, including the United States, Mexico, Russia, and India. There are also significant concerns about consumption of a genetically engineered, FDA-approved tomato produced by Calgene [a biotech company bought out by Monsanto in 1996] that contains an antibiotic-resistant gene that might confer resistance to common antibiotics used to treat children.

The increased creation, patenting, and use of genetically engineered plants and animals could also have a devastating impact on small farmers throughout the world. Only large, highly capitalized farms are likely to survive the increased overhead costs of growing and raising these patented organisms and the consequent price fluctuations caused by greater amounts of produce flooding the market. Moreover, new techniques in cloning tissue of various plants could eliminate outdoor farming of certain crops altogether. As noted by one economist, "Biotechnology will likely become dominant in the coming decades and will drive activities from the farm to the nonfarm sector at an increasing rate. . . . Full-time farming as we know it will cease to exist."

The controversy over genetically engineered animals and plants will certainly grow in the coming years, especially as more genetically engineered foods enter the global marketplace. Questions will continue to be raised about the unprecedented risks these organisms pose for human health and the environment, and society will increasingly confront the profound ethical concern over the appropriateness of unlimited cross-species genetic transfers and the patenting of life.

One powerful new community of resistance was announced on May 18, 1995. Nearly two hundred religious leaders announced their opposition to the patenting of animals and human materials. The unprecedented coalition included many Catholic bishops, along with leaders of most of the Protestant denominations and representatives of Jewish, Muslim, Buddhist, and Hindu groups. The published statement of the coalition of religious leaders was clear: "We believe that humans and animals are creations of God, not humans, and as such should not be patentable as human inventions." Southern Baptist leader Richard Land summed up the outrage of many religious leaders when he stated, "This [patenting] is not a slippery slope. This is a drop into the abyss. . . . We are seeing the ultimate commercial reduction of the very nature of human life and animal life."

Nevertheless, many in the science community and in the media remain undaunted in their support of the alteration and patenting of life. Over several years, the *New York Times* has several times singled out patenting opponents for editorial criticism. In a lead editorial entitled "Life, Industrialized," the *Times* succinctly stated a shockingly reductionist view of life perfectly suited to the new age of biocolonization: "Life is special, and humans even more so, but biological machines are still machines that now can be altered, cloned and patented. The consequences will be profound but taken a step at a time can be managed.". . .

A New Biodemocracy

On March 1, 1995, after six years of debate, the European Parliament (EP) rejected a European Union directive that would have allowed the patenting of virtually all life forms. The historic vote was a significant blow to life patenting in Europe and represents a surprise victory for "biodemocracy" and for ethics over profit. The action of the EP in rejecting life patents reflects the growing opposition that culminated in numerous street demonstrations in Brussels prior to the vote. For years, polls in Europe have shown overwhelming opposition to life patenting, especially animal and human materials patenting.

The U.S. Congress has taken no action against the engineering or patenting of life. However, polls of Americans show a high resistance to biotechnology. A 1992 USDA survey showed that 90 percent of those polled opposed the insertion of human genes into animals; 75 percent opposed the insertion of animal genes into plants; 60 percent opposed the insertion of foreign genes into animals; and over fifty percent felt that using biotechnology to change animals was "morally wrong."

About 80 percent felt that the public should have a greater voice in biotechnology decisions, believing that "citizens have too little to say about whether or not biotechnology should be used." This is a clear statement in favor of a new *biodemocracy*.

Biodemocracy requires that nation-states follow the example of the European Parliament and reject the patenting of life in all forms. It also requires governments and transnational corporations to stop biocolonizing the earth's genetic resources. . . . Finally, biodemocracy would lead to a moratorium on the engineering of the permanent genetic code of plants and animals. This work is potentially catastrophic for the environment and is profoundly unethical. Clearly, a mass movement for biodemocracy is needed if the international drive toward the engineering and patenting of life is to be halted. Biodemocracy involves respecting the collective will both to restrict biotechnology and to ban the patenting of life. It also involves the key ethical insight that all life forms have intrinsic value and genetic integrity and cannot be used as raw material for new commodities on the global market.

Dolly Ushers in the Age of Cloning

J. MADELEINE NASH

When the birth of Dolly, the world's first mammal cloned from an adult, was announced on February 22, 1997, cloning left the realm of science fiction and became a technical reality, generating massive international controversy that continues to this day. The existence of Dolly opened up a variety of scientific possibilities, from the creation of transgenic animals (which can be engineered to produce medicine or organs suitable for transplantation into humans), to the propagation of endangered animal species. Most controversially, Dolly also meant that human cloning was a technical possibility. Despite many beneficial possibilities, critics maintain that there are many risks associated with the cloning process, and some scientists claim that cloning necessarily produces an organism susceptible to premature aging. In fact, Dolly died on February 13, 2003, less than seven years after her birth on July 5, 1996, though it remains unclear whether this was due to her genesis as a clone. In the following selection J. Madeleine Nash, science and technology correspondent for Time *magazine, discusses the process used to clone Dolly, outlines the dangers involved with the process, and considers some of the ethical issues generated by this scientific milestone.*

E ven now, a week after news of the achievement first flew around the globe, traces of astonishment linger in the air like a contrail. The landmark paper published late last week [March 1997] in the journal *Nature* confirmed what the headlines had been screaming for days: researchers at the Roslin Institute near Edinburgh, Scotland, had indeed pulled off what many experts thought might be a scientific impossibility. From a cell in an adult ewe's mammary gland, embryologist Ian Wilmut and his colleagues managed to create a frisky lamb named Dolly (with apologies to Ms. Parton), scoring an advance in reproductive technology as unsettling as it was startling. Unlike offspring produced in the usual fashion, Dolly does not merely take after her biological mother. She is a carbon copy, a laboratory counterfeit so exact that she is in essence her mother's identical twin. What enabled the Scottish team to succeed where so many others have failed was a trick so ingenious, yet so simple, that any skilled laboratory technician should be able to master it—and therein lies both the beauty and the danger: once Wilmut and his colleagues figured out how to cross that biological barrier, they ensured that others would follow. And although the Roslin researchers had to struggle for more than 10 years to achieve their breakthrough, it took political and religious leaders around the world no time at all to grasp its import: If scientists can clone sheep, they can probably clone people too.

Without question, this exotic form of reproductive engineering could become an extremely useful tool. The ability to clone adult mammals, in particular, opens up myriad exciting possibilities, from propagating endangered animal species to producing replacement organs for transplant patients. Agriculture stands to benefit as well. Dairy farmers, for example, could clone their champion cows, making it possible to produce more milk from smaller herds. Sheep ranchers could do the same with their top lamb and wool producers.

But it's also easy to imagine the technology being misused, and as news from Roslin spread, apocalyptic scenarios proliferated. Journalists wrote seriously about the possibility of virgin births, resurrecting the dead and women giving birth to themselves. On the front page of the *New York Times*, a cell biologist from Washington University in St. Louis, Missouri, named Ursula Goodenough quipped that if cloning were perfected, "there'd be no need for men."

Scientists have long dreamed of doing what the Roslin team did. After all, if starfish and other invertebrates can practice asexual reproduction, why can't it be extended to the rest of the animal kingdom? In the 1980s, developmental biologists at what is now Allegheny University of the Health Sciences came tantalizingly close. From the red blood cells of an adult frog, they raised a crop of lively tadpoles. These tadpoles were impressive creatures, remembers University of Minnesota cell biologist Robert McKinnell, who followed the work closely. "They swam and ate and developed beautiful eyes and hind limbs," he says. But then, halfway through metamorphosis, they died.

Scientists who have focused their cloning efforts on more forgiving embryonic tissue have met with greater success. A simple approach, called embryo twinning (literally splitting embryos in half), is commonly practiced in the cattle industry. Coaxing surrogate cells to accept foreign DNA is a bit trickier. In 1952 researchers in Pennsylvania successfully cloned a live frog from an embryonic cell. Three decades later, researchers were learning to do the same with such mammals as sheep and calves. "What's new," observes University of Wisconsin animal scientist Neal First, "is not cloning mammals. It's cloning mammals from cells that are not embryonic."

Embryo cells are infinitely easier to work with because they are, in the jargon of cell biologists, largely "undifferentiated." That is, they have not yet undergone the progressive changes that turn cells into skin, muscles, hair, brain and so on. An undifferentiated cell can give rise to all the other cells in the body, say scientists, because it is capable of activating any gene on any chromosome. But as development progresses, differentiation alters the way DNA—the double-stranded molecule that makes up genes—folds up inside the nucleus of a cell. Along with other structural changes, folding helps make vast stretches of DNA inaccessible, ensuring that genes in adult cells do not turn on at the wrong time or in the wrong tissue.

The disadvantage of embryonic cloning is that you don't know what you are getting. With adult-cell cloning, you can wait to see how well an individual turns out before deciding whether to clone it. Cloning also has the potential to make genetic engineering more efficient. Once you produce an animal with a desired trait—a pig with a human immune system, perhaps—you could make as many copies as you want.

In recent years, some scientists have speculated that the changes wrought by differentiation might be irreversible, in which case cloning an adult mammal would be biologically impossible. The birth of Dolly not only proves them wrong but also suggests that the difficulty scientists have had cloning adult cells may have less to do with biology than with technique.

To create Dolly, the Roslin team concentrated on arresting the cell cycle—the series of choreographed steps all cells go through in the process of dividing. In Dolly's case, the cells the scientists wanted to clone came from the udder of a pregnant sheep. To stop them from dividing, researchers starved the cells of nutrients for a week. In response, the cells fell into a slumbering state that resembled deep hibernation.

At this point, Wilmut and his colleagues switched to a mainstream cloning technique known as nuclear transfer. First they removed the nucleus of an unfertilized egg, or oocyte, while leaving the surrounding cytoplasm intact. Then they placed the egg next to the nucleus of a quiescent donor cell and applied gentle pulses of electricity. These pulses prompted the egg to accept the new nucleus—and all the DNA it contained—as though it were its own. They also triggered a burst of biochemical activity, jumpstarting the process of cell division. A week later, the embryo that had already started growing into Dolly was implanted in the uterus of a surrogate ewe.

An inkling that this approach might work, says Wilmut, came from the success his team experienced in producing live lambs from embryonic clones. "Could we do it again with an adult cell?" wondered Wilmut, a reserved, self-deprecating man who likes gardening, hiking in the highlands and drinking good single-malt Scotch (but who was practical enough to file for a patent before he went public).

It was a high-risk project, and in the beginning Wilmut proceeded with great secrecy, limiting his core team to four scientists. His caution proved to be justified; the scientists failed far more often than they succeeded. Out of 277 tries, the researchers eventually produced only 29 embryos that survived longer than six days. Of these, all died before birth except Dolly, whose historic entry into the world was witnessed by a handful of researchers and a veterinarian.

Rumors that something had happened in Roslin, a small village in the green, rolling hills just south of Edinburgh, started circulating in scientific circles a few weeks ago [January 1997]. It was only last week, when the rumors were confirmed and the details of the experiment revealed, that the real excitement erupted. Cell biologists, like everybody else, were struck by the simple boldness of the experiment. But what intrigued them even more was what it suggested about how cells work.

Many scientists had suspected that the key to getting a donor cell and egg to dance together was synchronicity— getting them started on the same foot. Normal eggs and sperm don't have that problem; they come pre-divided, ready to combine. An adult cell, though, with its full complement of genes, has to be coaxed into entering an embryonic state. That is probably what Wilmut did by putting the donor cell to sleep, says Colin Stewart, an embryologist at the National Cancer Institute (NCI). Somehow, in ways scientists have yet to understand, this procedure seems to have reprogrammed the DNA of the donor cell. Thus when reawakened by the Roslin team, it was able to orchestrate the production of all the cells needed to make up Dolly's body.

Like most scientists who score major breakthroughs, Wilmut and his colleagues have raised more questions than they have answered. Among the most pressing are questions about Dolly's health. She is seven months old and appears to be perfectly fine, but no one knows if she will develop problems later on. For one thing, it is possible that Dolly may not live as long as other sheep. After all, observes NCI's Stewart, "she came from a six-year-old cell. Will she exhibit signs of aging prematurely?" In addition, as the high rate of spontaneous abortion suggests, cloning sometimes damages DNA. As a result, Dolly could develop any number of diseases that could shorten her life.

Indeed, cloning an adult mammal is still a difficult, cumbersome business—so much so that even agricultural and biomedical applications of the technology could be years away. PPL Therapeutics, the small biotechnical firm based in Edinburgh that provided a third of the funding to create Dolly, has its eye on the pharmaceutical market. Cloning, says PPL's managing director Ron James, could provide an efficient way of creating flocks of sheep that have been genetically engineered to produce milk laced with valuable enzymes and drugs. Among the pharmaceuticals PPL is looking at is a potential treatment for cystic fibrosis.

Nobody at Roslin or PPL is talking about cloning humans. Even if they were, their procedure is obviously not practical—not as long as dozens of surrogates need to be impregnated for each successful birth. And that is probably a good thing, because it gives the public time to digest the news—and policymakers time to find ways to prevent abuses without blocking scientific progress. If the policymakers succeed, and if their guidelines win international acceptance, it may take a lot longer than the editorial writers and talk-show hosts think before a human clone emerges—even from the shadows of some offshore renegade lab. "How long?" asks PPL's James. "Hopefully, an eternity."

Patenting Animal Genes Is Beneficial

U.S. PATENT AND TRADEMARK OFFICE

For the first two hundred years of the U.S. Patent and Trademark Office's existence, living organisms were excluded from patent laws as they were considered to be a "product of nature" and not a human invention. This changed in 1980, when justices in a landmark Supreme Court case (Diamond v. Chakrabarty) ruled that a strain of bacteria that had been genetically modified to break down hydrocarbons (it was hoped the bacteria would prove useful for cleaning up oil spills) was patentable because it was not naturally occurring. The decision sparked instant controversy and cleared the way for the patenting of more complex life forms.

The following selection has been excerpted from the guidelines on the patenting of genes, released by the U.S. Patent and Trademark Office (USPTO) on January 5, 2001. The guidelines address the agency's concerns raised during public debate over the patenting of genes. The main objections to gene patenting are that genes are discoveries and not inventions, that they represent a common natural heritage that cannot be owned, that gene patents are too broad, and that they hinder research. The USPTO counters that there is historical precedence for the granting of biological patents, that genetically modified organisms cannot be considered natural, and that patents actually encourage research. Moreover, the agency states, in granting gene patents it is adhering to laws passed by Congress.

U.S. Patent and Trademark Office, "Patent Applications—Utility Examination Guidelines," www.gpo.gov, January 5, 2001.

The Utility Requirement

Comment: Several comments state that while inventions are patentable, discoveries are not patentable. According to the comments, genes are discoveries rather than inventions. These comments urge the USPTO [United States Patent and Trademark Office] not to issue patents for genes on the ground that genes are not inventions.

Response: The suggestion is not adopted. An inventor can patent a discovery when the patent application satisfies the statutory requirements. The U.S. Constitution uses the word "discoveries" where it authorizes Congress to promote progress made by inventors. The pertinent part of the Constitution is Article 1, section 8, clause 8, which reads: "The Congress shall have power . . . To promote the Progress of Science and useful Arts, by securing for limited Times to Authors and Inventors the exclusive Right to their respective Writings and Discoveries."

When Congress enacted the patent statutes, it specifically authorized issuing a patent to a person who "invents or discovers" a new and useful composition of matter, among other things. The pertinent statute is 35 U.S.C. 101, which reads: "Whoever invents or discovers any new and useful process, machine, manufacture, or composition of matter, or any new and useful improvement thereof, may obtain a patent therefor, subject to the conditions and requirements of this title." Thus, an inventor's discovery of a gene can be the basis for a patent on the genetic composition isolated from its natural state and processed through purifying steps that separate the gene from other molecules naturally associated with it.

If a patent application discloses only nucleic acid molecular structure for a newly discovered gene, and no utility for the claimed isolated gene, the claimed invention is not patentable. But when the inventor also discloses how to use the purified gene isolated from its natural state, the application satisfies the "utility" requirement. That is, where the application discloses a specific, substantial, and credible utility for the claimed isolated and purified gene, the isolated and purified gene composition may be patentable.

Historical Precedents

Comment: Several comments state that a gene is not a new composition of matter because it exists in nature, and/or that an inventor who isolates a gene does not actually invent or discover a patentable composition because the gene exists in nature. These comments urge the USPTO not to issue patents for genes on the ground that genes are products of nature. Others state that naturally occurring DNAs are part of our heritage and are not inventions. Another comment expressed concern that a person whose body includes a patented gene could be guilty of patent infringement.

Response: The comments are not adopted. A patent claim directed to an isolated and purified DNA molecule could cover, e.g., a gene excised from a natural chromosome or a synthesized DNA molecule. An isolated and purified DNA molecule that has the same sequence as a naturally occurring gene is eligible for a patent because (1) an excised gene is eligible for a patent as a composition of matter or as an article of manufacture because that DNA molecule does not occur in that isolated form in nature, or (2) synthetic DNA preparations are eligible for patents because their purified state is different from the naturally occurring compound.

Patenting compositions or compounds isolated from nature follows well-established principles, and is not a new practice. For example, Louis Pasteur received U.S. Patent 141,072 in 1873, claiming "yeast, free from organic germs of disease, as an article of manufacture." Another example is an early patent for adrenaline. In a decision finding the patent valid, the court explained that compounds isolated from nature are patentable: "Even if it were merely an extracted product without change, there is no rule that such products are not patentable. [Japanese chemist Jokichi] Takamine was the first to make it [adrenaline] available for any use by removing it from the other gland-tissue in which it was found, and, while it is of course possible logically to call this a purification of the principle, it became for every practical purpose a new thing commercially and therapeutically. That was a good ground for a patent.". . .

A patent on a gene covers the isolated and purified gene but does not cover the gene as it occurs in nature. Thus, the concern that a person whose body "includes" a patented gene could infringe the patent is misfounded. The body does not contain the patented, isolated and purified gene because genes in the body are not in the patented, isolated and purified form. When the patent issued for purified adrenaline about one hundred years ago, people did not infringe the patent merely because their bodies naturally included unpurified adrenaline. . . .

The Question of Ownership

Comment: Several comments state that patents should not issue for genes because the sequence of the human genome is at the core of what it means to be human and no person should be able to own/control something so basic. Other comments stated that patents should be for marketable inventions and not for discoveries in nature.

Response: The comments are not adopted. Patents do not confer ownership of genes, genetic information, or sequences. The patent system promotes progress by securing a complete disclosure of an invention to the public, in exchange for the inventor's legal right to exclude other people from making, using, offering for sale, selling, or importing the composition for a limited time. That is, a patent owner can stop infringing activity by others for a limited time.

Discoveries from nature have led to marketable inventions in the past, but assessing the marketability of an invention is not pertinent to determining if an invention has a specific, substantial, and credible use. . . . Inventors are entitled to patents when they have met the statutory requirements for novelty, nonobviousness and usefulness, and their patent disclosure adequately describes the invention and clearly teaches others how to make and use the invention. The utility requirement, as explained by the courts, only requires that the inventor disclose a practical or real world benefit available from the invention, i.e., a specific, substantial and credible utility. As noted in a response to other comments, it is a long tradition in the United States that discoveries from nature which are transformed into new and useful products are eligible for patents.

Patents Encourage Research

Comment: Several comments state that the Guidelines mean that anyone who discovers a gene will be allowed a broad patent covering any number of possible applications even though those uses may be unattainable and unproven. Therefore, according to these comments, gene patents should not be issued.

Response: The comment is not adopted. When a patent claiming a new chemical compound issues, the patentee has the right to exclude others from making, using, offering for sale, selling, or importing the compound for a limited time. The patentee is required to disclose only one utility, that is, teach others how to use the invention in at least one way. The patentee is not required to disclose all possible uses, but promoting the subsequent discovery of other uses is one of the benefits of the patent system. When patents for genes are treated the same as for other chemicals, progress is promoted because the original inventor has the possibility to recoup research costs, because others are motivated to invent around the original patent, and because a new chemical is made available as a basis for future research. Other inventors who develop new and nonobvious methods of using the patented compound have the opportunity to patent those methods. . . .

Comment: Several comments state that patents should not issue for genes because patents on genes are delaying medical research and thus there is no societal benefit associated with gene patents. Others state that granting patents on genes at any stage of research deprives others of incentives and the ability to continue exploratory research and development. Some comment that patentees will deny access to genes and our property (our genes) will be owned by others.

Response: The comments are not adopted. The incentive to make discoveries and inventions is generally spurred, not inhibited, by patents. The disclosure of genetic inventions provides new opportunities for further development. The patent statutes provide that a patent must be granted when at least one specific, substantial and credible utility has been disclosed, and the application satisfies the other statutory requirements. As long as one specific, substantial and credible use is disclosed and the statutory requirements are met, the USPTO is not authorized to withhold the patent until another, or better, use is discovered. Other researchers may discover higher, better or more practical uses, but they are advantaged by the starting point that the original disclosure provides. A patent grants exclusionary rights over a patented composition but does not grant ownership of the composition. Patents are not issued on compositions in the natural environment but rather on isolated and purified compositions.

Congress Creates the Law

Comment: Several comments stated that DNA should be considered unpatentable because a DNA sequence by itself has little utility.

Response: A DNA sequence—i.e., the sequence of base pairs making up a DNA molecule—is simply one of the properties of a DNA molecule. Like any descriptive property, a DNA sequence itself is not patentable. A purified DNA molecule isolated from its natural environment, on the other hand, is a chemical compound and is patentable if all the statutory requirements are met. An isolated and purified DNA molecule may meet the statutory utility requirement if, e.g., it can be used to produce a useful protein or it hybridizes near and serves as a marker for a disease gene. Therefore, a DNA molecule is not per se unpatentable for lack of utility, and each application claim must be examined on its own facts. . . .

Comment: Several comments stated that DNA should be freely available for research. Some of these comments suggested that patents are not necessary to encourage additional discovery and sequencing of genes. Some comments suggested that patenting of DNA inhibits biomedical research by allowing a single person or company to control use of the claimed DNA. Another comment expressed concern that patenting ESTs [expressed sequence tags][1] will impede complete characterization of genes and delay or restrict exploration of genetic materials for the public good.

Response: The scope of subject matter that is eligible for a patent, the requirements that must be met in order to be granted a patent, and the legal rights that are conveyed by an issued patent, are all controlled by statutes which the USPTO must administer. "Whoever invents or discovers any new and useful . . . composition of matter . . . may obtain a patent therefor." Congress creates the law and the Federal judiciary interprets the law. The USPTO must administer the laws as Congress has enacted them and as the Federal courts have interpreted them. Current law provides that when the statutory patentability requirements are met, there is no basis to deny patent applications claiming DNA compositions, or to limit a patent's scope in order to allow free access to the use of the invention during the patent term.

1. short sections of DNA that are useful for identifying full-length genes

The Coming of Transgenic Farm Animals

SHELLEY SMITHSON

After decades of research, genetically engineered animals may soon pass through the regulatory net and enter the American food chain. The potential benefit of these animals is not limited to increased and economical food production. Transgenic animals could also be engineered to provide suitable organs for transplantation into humans, to produce protein-based drugs in their milk, or even to excrete industry-useful materials. In the following 2003 article freelance writer Shelley Smithson reports that many scientists believe that the regulatory body charged with deciding how safe these animals would be to eat, the U.S. Food and Drug Administration (FDA), has neither the qualifications nor the legal authority to adequately evaluate and regulate the most recent advances in the genetic engineering of animals. Furthermore, because of the regulatory scheme the FDA is using, the agency cannot reveal the names of the companies involved in creating transgenic animals, the details of the genetic alterations, or the potential health effects these animals may have when eaten until the product has been approved. Despite fierce objections from many scientists, these animals are likely to become part of America's diet.

Last January [2003], inspectors with the U.S. Food and Drug Administration [FDA] paid a visit to the University of Illinois, where researchers have been studying the DNA of pigs. The pig project, based in Champaign-Urbana, is one of dozens of experiments being conducted across the country in which scientists are altering the genetic structure of animals in hopes of making them fatter, healthier, and more profitable.

In the University of Illinois project, cow genes were inserted into sows to increase their milk production, and a synthetic gene was added to make milk digestion easier for the piglets, thereby causing them to grow faster. But instead of the experimental swine being destroyed, as required by the FDA, 386 piglets were sold to livestock brokers, who then sold them to slaughterhouses, who sold them to grocery stores, who sold them to consumers as pork chops, sausage, and bacon.

An Outdated Regulatory System

University officials claim the piglets did not inherit the genetic baggage of their moms, and the government does not believe the incident presented a public-health risk. But the slipup is emblematic of a federal regulatory system that is behind the times when it comes to the next phase of bioengineered food: genetically modified [GM] animals.

[Since the late 1990s], GM soybeans and corn have become mainstays in processed food sold in the United States, despite nagging questions about the safety of the products and their potential capacity to cause ecological harm. Now, scientists, environmentalists, and food-safety advocates are concerned that GM meat, eggs, and milk could follow in the footsteps of transgenic crops, becoming a part of the U.S. diet before they have been shown to be safe for humans, animals, and the environment.

Universities and biotechnology companies are conducting experiments that mix and match genes from different organisms to produce animals that could not occur in nature: bioengineered salmon that grow five times as fast as their wild cousins, hens genetically manipulated to lay low-cholesterol eggs, cows with disease-resistant genes, chickens that produce anti-cancer drugs. Some say this work holds great promise for preventing disease, boosting agricultural productivity, and eradicating world hunger. But public-interest groups worry that in the absence of a unified regulatory system, the patchwork of outdated rules applied by different federal agencies could jeopardize food safety and the environment.

No Drug-Style Reviews

To date, no GM animals have been approved for sale within the U.S. food industry, and it will probably be several years before genetically modified eggs, milk, and meat make their way into U.S. grocery stores and restaurants. The FDA is currently reviewing 10 applications from companies seeking to sell GM animal products to consumers—but rather than evaluating these products as food, the FDA is reviewing them under the rules that govern new drugs for animals. The agency reasons that adding a foreign substance—genes from another organism or synthetic genes—to an animal's DNA is similar to feeding the animal a drug because it creates a physical change in the animal, such as faster growth or disease resistance.

Jane Rissler, a senior staff scientist for the Union of Concerned Scientists [UCS], calls the use of the drug rule to regulate GM animals a "contortion." Rissler spent four years at the U.S. EPA [Environmental Protection Agency] helping to formulate biotechnology regulations before joining UCS, a Cambridge, Mass.–based nonprofit [organization], in 1993. She is concerned about the use of the drug law to regulate GM animals because it "is weak on the environment and it allows zero public participation."

Under the animal drug law, the FDA cannot discuss anything about the GM animal products currently being reviewed—not the names of the companies involved, the types of animals being modified, the ways their genetic structures have been altered, or the potential effects on food safety, animal health, or the environment. "We cannot reveal that type of information. It's considered a violation of our rules," says Linda Grassie, an FDA spokesperson. The agency will issue a report on its findings only after a product has been approved and gone on the market.

By contrast, when Procter & Gamble, the makers of Olestra, asked the FDA for permission to add its artificial fat substitute to potato chips, the controversial product was evaluated under food-additive laws. In that process, the FDA files a notice in the Federal Register and public-interest groups collect and present scientific data to the FDA in writing and at open hearings.

The secretive process now being used to review GM animals is at odds with what the American people seem to want. A 2001 survey conducted by the Pew Initiative on Food and Biotechnology indicated that people desire more information about GM food. Sixty-five percent of respondents were concerned about eating bioengineered food and 45 percent lacked confidence in the government's ability to ensure the safety of such food.

"A large element of what people are looking for with this technology is having a process that is not only scientifically sound, but having a process that the public can trust," says Michael Taylor, former deputy commissioner for policy at the FDA. "That transparency is an important part of public confidence in the outcome."

Taylor was a contributing author to a 2002 National Academy of Sciences report on GM animals that noted several food-safety concerns, including allergies, digestive disorders, and antibiotic resistance. According to the report, people with weak digestive systems—such as those with gastroenteritis—could absorb whole proteins into their blood streams, potentially causing allergic reactions. Infants in particular could be threatened, because their digestive systems are not fully developed. But people with healthy digestive tracts also could be at risk: "Food products containing antimicrobial proteins might present a food safety concern in view of their potential to alter the balance of consumers' intestinal flora, and might foster the evolution of microbial strains resistant to specific agents," the report says.

Cheap Salmon at What Price?

Many scientists also worry about the ecological effects of tinkering with the genetic structure of animals. On the bright side, some environmental problems could be mitigated by bioengineered animals, such as pigs that produce low-phosphorus poop (which would cut down on emissions of methane, a greenhouse gas) and fluorescent, color-coded fish that would indicate the presence of different water pollutants.

But there is concern that GM animals, especially fish, could escape from holding pens and breed with wild populations, causing dramatic shifts in ecosystems. Scientists at Purdue University in West Lafayette, Ind., described a scenario in which fish engineered to grow faster would compete with wild fish for food and mating partners, potentially driving them to extinction. Opponents of genetic modification worry that a bioengineered salmon currently being reviewed by the FDA could cause Atlantic salmon, already listed as an endangered species, to become extinct.

"In return for possibly slightly cheaper salmon, you run the risk of wiping out wild salmon populations," says Jean Halloran, director of the Consumer Policy Institute at Consumers Union, the New York research institute that publishes *Consumer Reports*. "Yeah, I guess it would be an advantage if [salmon] were cheaper, but at what price?"

Under the current rules, the FDA—not the EPA—is responsible for environmental assessments of GM animal projects; these assessments are also conducted without public input. "The FDA is absolutely not qualified to regulate the environmental risks of any animals," Rissler says.

"They are not environmental specialists." The EPA studies the environmental risks posed by GM crops, and Rissler says the agency should also assess the potential ecological impacts of bioengineered animals, because its scientists have the expertise to ask the right questions.

The FDA insists it is qualified, even though its primary mission is not environmental regulation. "When we have expertise deficiencies in a particular area, we go out and get experts," says John Matheson, a senior regulatory review scientist for the FDA's Center for Veterinary Medicine. Matheson, who is an aquatic ecologist, says that in the case of the GM salmon, the FDA is working with the EPA and the U.S. Fish and Wildlife Service to conduct a thorough review. However, according to the National Academy of Sciences report, the FDA does not have the legal authority to deny a GM animal application based on an environmental assessment.

Just Eat It?

Until the glitch at the University of Illinois was discovered a few months ago [in 2003], the FDA did not require researchers to inform them that they were conducting GM animal experiments. Nor did they make it clear to research organizations that GM animals could not be sold into the commercial food supply. In fact, the Illinois researchers were working closely with the FDA, and still did not understand the rules governing their experimental animals.

In May, the FDA sent a letter to all land-grant universities reminding researchers that their work "may require" licensing under the animal drug law. "Because much is yet to be learned about the positive and negative facets of this type of research, it is imperative that all safety regulations be followed scrupulously," the FDA letter admonished. That seems like a reasonable request—but, as Halloran of Consumers Union puts it, "I can't imagine how a researcher would know what the rules are, because they don't exist in writing."

The agency is hoping to have voluntary guidelines for applicants completed within a year, the FDA's Matheson says. "With animal biotech, there's such a diversity; it's hard to anticipate the next one to come in the door," he says. Because the technology is new, "we're not yet in a place to decide in stone what kind of requirements might be applied."

Public-interest groups say it's time for the FDA to start deciding. They're calling on the agency to develop regulations specifically for bioengineered food products rather than trying to adapt old rules, intended for conventional food and drugs, to a radically new technology. These new regulations, they say, could spell out the roles of different federal agencies and could require applicants to follow specific testing criteria on matters such as sample sizes and duration of experiments. They also could outline a public participation process and require the labeling of products containing genetically engineered organisms—something that is not now done.

"The public is currently in the situation of not even having awareness that anyone is thinking about genetically engineering animals for human consumption," Halloran says. "And the way the structure is currently set up, that's going to go on until one day the FDA says, 'We've just approved a genetically engineered animal and we're not going to label it. So, here it is; eat it.'"

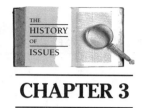

CHAPTER 3

Engineered Humans

Chapter Preface

Fears about the genetic engineering of humans developed long before the technology to do so had even begun to be developed. These concerns arose after the publication of various writings, such as Aldous Huxley's 1930 novel *Brave New World,* which described a future society in which humans were created in vast fertility laboratories and manipulated to develop into perfect specimens for predetermined social roles. What most concerned people who read such writings were their suggestion that it might one day be possible to design people with specific characteristics.

Indeed, from its beginning, the debate over the genetic engineering of humans has been linked with the controversial field of eugenics. Eugenics, an idea developed in the latter half of the nineteenth century, was the science of improving the human race by selective breeding. While eugenics had received serious scientific attention for decades prior to World War II, its association with Nazi ideology in the 1930s and 1940s had widely discredited the concept as socially unacceptable. Beginning with the sterilization of the handicapped and ending with the Holocaust, Nazi leader Adolf Hitler sought to create a superior Aryan race through the elimination of genetically "inferior" humans from the gene pool. The association of genetic engineering with eugenics is still strong in the public's mind.

Critics of engineering humans argue that any form of genetic modification of humans is a form of eugenics. They worry that manipulation of human traits would essentially alter what it means to be human, thereby devaluing the individual. Opponents say that such tampering with human genes is playing God. Many critics also contend that engineering humans will lead to greater social inequity. They point out that only the affluent would be able to afford genetic enhancements of their children, leaving the poor to compete with smarter, more attractive people. In contrast, proponents of the technology argue that human genetic engineering could lead to the eradication of inheritable diseases. Some go further and argue that genetic technologies should be used to improve human characteristics, such as intelligence or physical prowess, in an effort to provide humanity with an evolutionary advantage. They maintain that there is nothing inherently unethical about this, as it ultimately benefits everyone.

Whether the genetic manipulation of humans will result in the eradication of inheritable diseases and make humanity more successful, or whether such engineering of character traits will lead to a devaluation of the individual and increased social inequality remains to be seen. Although it is too soon to tell whether Huxley's grim vision of an engineered society will become reality, clearly he was prophetic in envisioning the role that genetic engineering might play in humanity's future.

The Patenting of Human Genes Restricts Research

ARTHUR ALLEN

Begun in 1990, the Human Genome Project (HGP) is an on-going international effort to identify the complete sequence of the three billion DNA base pairs in the human genome, and to map all of its twenty to twenty-five thousand genes. One of the issues that arose from the HGP was the question of who owns biological information. This question became the center of a controversy one year after the beginning of the project when, in 1991, the National Institutes of Health (which were responsible for planning and developing the project) applied for patents on over seven thousand fragments of DNA. One of the more controversial aspects of the patent claims was that the claimants did not understand what the functions of the sequences were, and the patent claims were ultimately rejected by the U.S. Patent and Trademark Office for this reason. This was not the end of the issue, however.

In 1992 the researcher responsible for the technique that allowed the HGP to map sequences with increasing efficiency and speed, Craig Venter, left the project to launch the privately funded Institute for Genomic Research, which began competing with the government's effort to decode human DNA. The database compiled by Venter was soon bought by U.S. drug company SmithKline Beecham, which granted scientists access to it only if they agreed to concede rights to any patentable discovery. The corporation's actions worried many in the scientific community, who believed the company was trying to monopolize the human genome. The race to patent genetic information was on, with private companies soon claiming thousands of patents on whole or partial genes. These patents are extremely valuable, as one gene patent has the potential to be used for a wide range of applications, from diagnostic tests to gene therapies to future pharmaceutical products. In the following 2000 article Arthur Allen, health and science writer for the online magazine Salon, *argues that human genome patents are hindering the research and use of medical techniques that could otherwise save lives.*

For years, the parents of children suffering from an implacable genetic disorder called Canavan disease dutifully packed off their blood and tissue samples to Dr. Reuben Matalon, a researcher at Miami Children's Hospital. These shipments were an altruistic, volunteer effort by a devastated group of people—their own children were dead or dying, but they hoped to prevent the births of more children with the disastrous, inevitably fatal brain disease.

In 1993, their donations paid off when Matalon, parsing the families' DNA, was able to identify a series of gene mutations on chromosome 17 that appeared to indirectly cause the disease, which has mainly affected Ashkenazi [eastern European] Jews. His work raised hopes that Canavan would go the way of Tay-Sachs, a related illness that has nearly disappeared in the Jewish population since couples began routine screening for Tay-Sachs in the early 1970s.

The Cost of Information

But the Tay-Sachs screening program, apparently, belonged to a kinder, gentler era in medicine. In November 1998, Miami Children's Hospital announced plans to strictly license its patent on the Canavan gene. Not only did Miami Children's demand that clinicians pay a $25 royalty (eventually lowered to $12.50) each time they performed the test; it also put a cap on the number of tests any academic lab could do.

The hospital's stringent licensing agreement is part of an alarming trend in biomedical research. Some biotech companies, universities and even hospitals are seeking to recoup their costs quickly by patenting discoveries that many believe shouldn't be patented at all. The patent license disputes threaten to close off research and clinical applications of some of the biomedical discoveries that Americans have paid billions to enable.

Some of the leading genetics labs in the country would not accept Miami Children's licensing terms and as a result had to stop testing for Canavan disease. "It's a wretched contract and we refused to sign it," says Debra Leonard, director of the molecular pathology laboratory at the University of Pennsylvania hospitals in Philadelphia. Shocked patient groups and scientists could only watch in dismay as bickering lawyers put a squeeze on information they'd worked long and hard to generate.

Restricted Access

"We gave our DNA and that of our children to help develop testing and prenatal diagnosis. We sent our blood and skin samples to a doctor at Miami Children's Hospital," says Dr. Judith Tsipis, a Brandeis University biologist whose son, Andreas, died of Canavan disease in 1998 at age 22. "Is it right that they use our genes—given to help others—in a way that restricts access and increases cost to testing?

"It's shocking," she says.

"My understanding from the hospital was we needed to file the patent just so I could work with the gene myself," says Matalon, who has since moved to the University of Texas hospital system, where he continues to work on Canavan disease. "I had nothing to do with their licensing decision and I got no penny from any patent."

Canavan disease is one of a growing number of conditions in which patent fights have intruded into genetic medicine. Ninety percent of the 150 U.S. clinical genetics labs in a recent survey reported having withheld tests because of onerous patent claims. Genes for early-onset Alzheimer's and breast cancer are among the most common DNA sequences saddled with restrictive licenses.

Doctors whose clinical practice involves devising means to detect disease-causing genetic mutations are being told they can only perform such tests under licensing agreements that are often so strict the doctors' institutions refuse to sign them.

"This is my medical practice. I can't do what I was trained to do, and I spent a long time training to do it," says Leonard, who is also president of the Association for Molecular Pathology.

The Decoding of DNA

The problem will only grow with the approval of thousands of additional gene applications currently pending before the U.S. Patent and Trade Office. "This is just the tip of the iceberg," says Leonard. The conflicts over genetic testing—the first clinical application of the Human Genome Project—are probably just an opening skirmish in a multisided war for control of the information, drugs and therapies that may arise from the genome discoveries.

Thanks to robots, supercomputers and brainy scientists, the government-led genome project is expected this year or next [2000–2001] to finish its sequencing of the estimated 100,000 genes in human DNA.[1] But the mapping of the human chromosomes is really just the start of a new kind of biological understanding. Although scientists now know the DNA sequences of many human genes, they don't understand how most of them work.

While the rest of us await the integration of these molecules into an intelligible language of life, scientists, businessmen and the government squabble over what value to

1. When the project published the finished sequence on October 20, 2004, it was discovered that there were only twenty thousand to twenty-five thousand genes, an unexpectedly low number.

assign the millions of information snippets.

James Watson, who won the Nobel Prize in 1953 for discovering DNA's double-helix structure, resigned as the first director of the NIH [National Institutes of Health] genome institute in 1992 in a dispute over whether to patent DNA sequences that a scientist named Craig Venter had discovered. Venter also quit the NIH and formed a gene sequencing partnership with William Haseltine, a Harvard AIDS scientist. Haseltine and Venter now lead competing biotech firms that are racing a government-led consortium to decode vast quantities of human DNA.

A Plausible Function

Haseltine, Venter and other scientific entrepreneurs have submitted patent applications on millions of bits of DNA, many of whose function isn't clearly understood. The patent office recently raised the bar of knowledge it requires before issuing patents on genes, but Francis Collins, Watson's successor, worries that premature claim-staking on the genome could end up snarling research in legal battles for years.

Using the sophisticated databanks, most of them designed and run by the government, genome-analyzing companies have described possible functions for about half the gene sequences discovered so far. John Doll, who heads the U.S. Patent and Trade Office's biotechnology division, says his office will grant patents for genes when applicants can describe a plausible function for them based on computer searches.

A prime example was the patent awarded [in February 2000] to Human Genome Sciences for a gene that codes for a protein involved in introducing the HIV virus into cells. When Haseltine filed for the patent in 1995, he didn't know the function of the gene, but was savvy enough to guess it might be a cell membrane receptor. In the meantime, AIDS researchers doing painstaking science uncovered the actual role of the gene. The awarding of the patent—worth millions if the gene is used to create AIDS drugs or vaccines—infuriated these scientists as well as patient groups that supported their research.

"Doesn't it bother you," Collins asked Doll during a conference in Washington . . . , "that your standard would allow patent protection for roughly 40 percent of human genes, and yet if you ask any working scientist what percent of human genes they know the function of, you'd get maybe 2 percent?"

"Everybody's filing for these patents," said Doll. "Not just the Incytes of the world; zillions of universities are taking the same approach."

"I don't doubt it for a second but it doesn't make me feel any different," an exasperated Collins responded. "When there's a gold rush, a lot of people go to California."

The Gathering of Biological Information

Other scientists are less restrained in their attacks on the biotech industry. "The idea of patenting DNA sequences is abhorrent to me, but in particular, the way it's being done now is intellectually dishonest," says Robert Nussbaum, a molecular biologist at NIH.

Nussbaum, who works on Parkinson's disease, said the kind of gene patent applications that Doll's office has decided to approve are likely to be shaky in their claims. Even if correct, he said, such claims are based on searches of public databases and "are being done on the backs and shoulders of research funded by the public and charitable foundations. It doesn't seem right that these sequences should be taken and locked up for the purpose of profit making."

Doll points out that hard work has never been a requirement to win a patent from the U.S. Patent Office, which generally tries to be as friendly to patent applicants as possible. "We don't care how you find out something new, only that you're the first to find it," he says. And some biotech officials say that scientists are simply bitter at the fact that technology is transforming the manner in which biological information is gathered.

Officials at Incyte, a Palo Alto, Calif., company that sells its genome information to more than two dozen pharmaceutical and biotech companies, like to point to a discovery made [in 1999] by CV Therapeutics, a small California biotech company. Using Incyte's databases and a few simple experiments, scientists from CV Therapeutics were able to identify a set of genes involved in Tangier disease, a heart ailment discovered among people living on Tangier Island in the Chesapeake Bay. CV's discovery took two months, but it was listed by the American Heart Association as one of the top 10 discoveries of 1999.

"Medical research is increasingly a matter of using technologies to gather a bunch of pieces of information," says Lee Bendekgey, general counsel for Incyte. "It's really accelerating things and that's what matters. And when people make discoveries like that, they deserve both public accolades and rewards."

Intellectual Property

In the 1980s, in a more primitive era of genetics discoveries, it took Francis Collins several years to isolate and clone the cystic fibrosis gene. At the time it was one of the more remarkable chapters in genetics research. The University of Michigan, where Collins made the discovery, holds the patent on the gene. As it happens, Michigan doesn't charge researchers a dime to use it.

Of course, patent holders want people to use their inventions—if no one uses them, they don't get paid. And intellectual property lawyers say that when the patents on the human genome get sorted out, relevant ones will be bundled into packages that can be licensed to researchers and doctors in useable form—for a price.

When the Human Genome Project began, ethicists were primarily worried about whether knowledge from the genome would be used for genetic discrimination, or to create genetically enhanced children or eliminate the genetically unfit. But such concerns may be beside the point if the technology is too expensive for anyone but the rich.

Those who care for the genetically vulnerable appear most aware of this paradox. Judith Tsipis' son Andreas never learned to walk, talk or feed himself. But he could think—and he had a good sense of humor, she says. Asked the difficult question of whether Andreas' birth should never have taken place, Tsipis shrugs off facile answers.

"Andreas was my child and I loved him dearly. He was loved and cared for superbly well but he still had a difficult life, especially toward the end. Would I have wanted him to be born? I can't answer that. But I'm working very hard for screening so that families have all the options, and one option is an abortion. The key thing you need is information, education, and the availability of testing."

"If patents hinder research," she adds, "it will make it harder for people to develop cures for these diseases."

A Gene Therapy Trial Fails: The Death of Jesse Gelsinger

SHERYL GAY STOLBERG

Gene therapy is an experimental technique that seeks to correct a genetic disease in an individual by providing the body with the genetic information it lacks. This is typically achieved through the introduction of a genetically engineered virus that delivers a good copy of a specific gene into a cell that contains a defective gene in an attempt to restore the patient's normal functions. On September 14, 1990, the first human gene therapy experiment was conducted by U.S. geneticist W. French Anderson on four-year-old Ashanti Desilva. Although the experiment did not yield a complete cure, it was successful in alleviating Desilva's immunodeficiency, leading many researchers to speculate on the future possibilities of this new technique.

Although gene therapy showed great promise, researchers were divided about the ethics of pushing forward with human tests. These reservations were quickly shown to be warranted. On November 28, 1999, the first death directly related to gene therapy occurred. Volunteer patient Jesse Gelsinger reacted negatively to an experimental infusion of a gene that doctors hoped would help treat a rare metabolic disorder called ornithine transcarbamylase (OTC). As **New York**

Times *health and medicine writer Sheryl Gay Stolberg notes in the following selection from 1999, Gelsinger's death brought the issue of gene therapy to the public's attention, touching off a debate over the safety of the technology. Although gene therapy trials continued, scientists faced another major setback in January 2003, when twenty-seven U.S. trials were halted after two children treated in France developed a condition resembling leukemia.*

As far as government officials know, [Jesse Gelsinger's] death on Sept. 17 [1999] was the first directly related to gene therapy. The official cause, as listed on the death certificate filed by [surgeon Steve] Raper, was adult respiratory distress syndrome: his lungs shut down. The truth is more complicated. Jesse's therapy consisted of an infusion of corrective genes, encased in a dose of weakened cold virus, adenovirus, which functioned as what scientists call a vector. Vectors are like taxicabs that drive healthy DNA into cells; viruses, whose sole purpose is to get inside cells and infect them, make useful vectors. The Penn [University of Pennsylvania] researchers had tested their vector, at the same dose Jesse got, in mice, monkeys, baboons and one human patient, and had seen expected, flulike side effects, along with some mild liver inflammation, which disappeared on its own. When Jesse got the vector, he suffered a chain reaction that the testing had not predicted—jaundice, a blood-clotting disorder, kidney failure, lung failure and brain death: in Raper's words, "multiple-organ-system failure." The doctors are still investigating; their current hypothesis is that the adenovirus triggered an overwhelming inflammatory reaction—in essence, an immune-system revolt. What they do not understand yet is why.

Not Yet Therapy

Every realm of medicine has its defining moment, often with a human face attached. Polio had Jonas Salk. In vitro fertilization had Louise Brown, the world's first test-tube baby. Transplant surgery had Barney Clark, the Seattle dentist with the artificial heart. AIDS had Magic Johnson. Now gene therapy has Jesse Gelsinger.

Until Jesse died, gene therapy was a promising idea that had so far failed to deliver. As scientists map the human genome, they are literally tripping over mutations that cause rare genetic disorders, including OTC deficiency, Jesse's disease. The initial goal was simple: to cure, or prevent, these illnesses by replacing defective genes with healthy ones. Biotech companies have poured millions into research—not for rare hereditary disorders but for big-profit illnesses like cancer, heart disease and AIDS. As of August [1999], the government had reviewed 331 gene-therapy protocols involving more than 4,000 patients. Just 41 were for the "monogeneic," or single-gene, defect diseases whose patients so desperately hoped gene therapy would be their salvation.

At the same time, the science has progressed slowly, researchers have had trouble devising vectors that can carry genes to the right cells and get them to work once they are there. [In 1995], Dr. Harold Varmus, the director of the National Institutes of Health [N.I.H.], commissioned a highly critical report about gene therapy, chiding investigators for creating "the mistaken and widespread perception of success." Since then, there have been some accomplishments: a team at Tufts University has used gene therapy to grow new blood vessels for heart disease patients, for instance. But so far, gene therapy has not cured anyone. As Ruth Macklin, a bioethicist and member of the Recombinant DNA Advisory Committee, the National Institutes of Health panel that oversees gene-therapy research, says, bluntly, "Gene therapy is not yet therapy."

Safety Concerns

On Dec. 8 [1999], the "RAC," as the committee is called, will begin a public inquiry into Jesse's death, as well as the safety of adenovirus, which has been used in roughly one-quarter of all gene-therapy clinical trials. The Penn scientists will report on their preliminary results, and investigators, who at the RAC's request have submitted thousands of pages of patient safety data to the committee, will discuss the side effects of adenovirus. Among them will be researchers from the Schering-Plough Corporation, which was running two experiments in advanced liver cancer patients that used methods similar to Penn's. Enrollment in those trials was suspended by the Food and Drug Administration [F.D.A.] after Jesse's death. The company, under pressure from the RAC, has since released information showing that some patients experienced serious side effects, including changes in liver function and blood-cell counts, mental confusion and nausea; two experienced minor strokes, although one had a history of them. Once all the data on adenovirus are analyzed at the Dec. 8 meeting, the RAC may recommend restrictions on its use, which will almost certainly slow down some aspects of gene-therapy research.[1]

The meeting will be important for another reason: it will mark an unprecedented public airing of information about the safety of gene therapy—precisely the kind of sharing the RAC has unsuccessfully sought in the past. Officials say gene therapy has claimed no lives besides Jesse's. But since his death, there have been news reports that other patients died during the course of experiments—from their diseases, as opposed to the therapy—and that the scientists involved did not report those deaths to the RAC, as is required. This has created a growing cloud of suspicion over gene therapy, raising questions about whether other scientists may have withheld information that could have prevented Jesse's death. That question cannot be answered until all the data are analyzed. But one thing is certain: four years after the field was rocked by Varmus's highly critical evaluation, it is now being rocked again, this

1. Although gene therapy trials were allowed to continue, researchers were criticized for failing to report adverse events in clinical trials and are now governed by tighter regulations.

time over an issue more fundamental than efficacy—safety.

"I think it's a perilous time for gene therapy," says LeRoy Walters, a bioethicist at Georgetown University and former chairman of the RAC. "Until now, we have been able to say, 'Well, it hasn't helped many people, but at least it hasn't hurt people.' That has changed.". . .

Human Testing

Gene therapy became a reality on Sept. 14, 1990, in a hospital room at the National Institutes of Health, in Bethesda, Md., when a 4-year-old girl with a severe immune-system deficiency received a 30-minute infusion of white blood cells that had been engineered to contain copies of the gene she lacked. Rarely in modern medicine has an experiment been filled with so much hope; news of the treatment ricocheted off front pages around the world. The scientist who conducted it, Dr. W. French Anderson, quickly became known as the father of gene therapy. "We had got ourselves all hyped up," Anderson now admits, "thinking there would be rapid, quick, easy, early cures.". . .

There had been some early problems with safety—a 1993 cystic fibrosis experiment was shut down when a patient was hospitalized with inflamed lungs—but doctors Jim Wilson and Mark Batshaw say they figured out how to make a safer vector by deleting extra viral genes. Adenovirus was the right size: when its viral genes were excised, the OTC gene fit right in. It had a "ZIP code," on it, Batshaw says, that would carry it straight to the liver. And while its effects did not last, it worked quickly, which meant that it might be able to reverse a coma, sparing babies from brain damage. "It wasn't going to be a cure soon," Batshaw says, "but it might be a treatment soon."

The mouse experiments were encouraging. Mice that had the therapy survived for two to three months even while fed a high-protein diet. Those that lacked the treatment died. "It wasn't subtle," Wilson says. "We felt pretty compelled by that." But when the team contemplated testing in people, they ran smack into an ethical quandary: who should be their subjects?

To Wilson, the answer seemed obvious: sick babies. Arthur Caplan, the university's resident bioethics expert, thought otherwise. Caplan says parents of dying infants are incapable of giving informed consent: "They are coerced by the disease of their child." He advised Wilson to test only stable adults, either female carriers or men like Jesse, with partial enzyme deficiencies. The National Urea Cycle Disorders Foundation agreed. When Batshaw turned up at their 1994 annual meeting asking for volunteers, so many mothers offered to be screened for the OTC gene that it took him four hours to draw all the blood.

By the time Mark Batshaw and Jim Wilson submitted their experiment to the Recombinant DNA Advisory Committee for approval, the panel was in danger of being disbanded. Varmus, the N.I.H. director, who won the Nobel Prize for his discovery of a family of cancer-causing genes, had made no secret of this distaste for the conduct of gene-therapy researchers. He thought the science was too shoddy to push forward with human testing, and it bothered him that so few experiments were focusing on genetic diseases. It irked him to have to sign off on protocols the RAC approved, and it irked him even more to see biotech companies touting those approvals, like some kind of N.I.H. imprimatur, in the business pages of the paper. "Some days," says Dr. Nelson Wivel, the committee's former executive director, who now works for Wilson at Penn, "it felt as though the RAC was helping the biotech industry raise money. Dr. Varmus hated that.". . .

"The Maximum Tolerated Dose"

The Batshaw-Wilson protocol was among the last the committee would ever approve. The plan was for 18 adults (19 eventually signed up, including Tish Simon [cofounder of the National Urea Cycle Foundation], but the last patient was never treated, because of Jesse's death) to receive an infusion of the OTC gene, tucked inside an adenovirus vector, through a catheter in the hepatic artery, which leads to the liver. The goal was to find what Wilson calls "the maximum tolerated dose," one high enough to get the gene to work, but low enough to spare patients serious side effects. Subjects would be split into six groups of three, with each group receiving a slightly higher dose than the last. This is standard fare in safety testing. "You go up in small-enough increments," Wilson explains, "that you can pull the plug on the thing before people get hurt."

The experiment stood in stark contrast to others that had earned Varmus's scorn. It was paid for by N.I.H., which meant it had withstood the rigors of scientific peer review. It was aimed at a rare genetic disease, not cancer or AIDS. It was supported by plenty of animal research: Wilson and his team had performed more than 20 mouse experiments to test efficacy and a dozen safety studies on mice, rhesus monkeys and baboons. Still, it made [geneticist Robert] Erickson, one of two scientists assigned by the RAC to review the experiment, uneasy.

He was troubled by data showing that three monkeys had died of a blood-clotting disorder and severe liver inflammation when they received an earlier, stronger version of the adenovirus vector at a dose 20 times the highest dose planned for the study. No one had injected adenovirus directly into the bloodstream before, either via the liver or otherwise, and the scientists admitted that it was difficult to tell precisely how people would respond. They planned to confine the infusion to the right lobe of the liver, so that if damage occurred it would be contained there, sparing the left lobe. And they outlined the major risks: bleeding, from either the gene-therapy site or a subsequent liver biopsy, which would require surgery; or serious liver inflammation, which could require an organ transplant and might lead to death.

Both Erickson and the other scientific reviewer thought the experiment was too risky to test on asymptomatic volunteers and recommended rejection. But in the end, Batshaw and Wilson prevailed. They offered up Caplan's argument that testing on babies was inappropriate. And they agreed to inject the vector into the bloodstream, as opposed to putting it directly into the liver. That decision, however, was later reversed by the F.D.A., which insisted that because the adenovirus would travel through the blood and wind up in the liver anyway, the original plan was safer.

The RAC, in such disarray from Varmus's reorganization that it did not meet again for another year, was never informed of the change.

Jesse Gelsinger was 17 when his pediatric geneticist, Dr. Randy Heidenreich, first told him about the Penn proposal. He wanted to sign up right away. But he had to wait until he was 18. . . .

Jesse Enrolls

The treatment began on Monday, Sept. 13. Jesse would receive the highest dose. Seventeen patients had already been treated, including one woman who had been given the same dose that Jesse would get, albeit from a different lot, and had done "quite well," Raper says. That morning, Jesse was taken to the interventional-radiology suite, where he was sedated and strapped to a table while a team of radiologists threaded two catheters into his groin. At 10:30 A.M., Raper drew 30 milliliters of the vector and injected it slowly. At half past noon, he was done. . . .

Early Tuesday morning a nurse called Raper at home; Jesse seemed disoriented. When Raper got to the hospital, about 6:15 A.M., he noticed that the whites of Jesse's eyes were yellow. That meant jaundice, not a good sign. "It was not something we had seen before," Raper says. A test confirmed that Jesse's bilirubin, a breakdown product of red blood cells, was four times the normal level. Raper called [Paul] Gelsinger [Jesse's father], and Batshaw in Washington, who said he would get on a train and be there in two hours.

Both doctors knew that the high bilirubin meant one of two things: either Jesse's liver was failing or he was suffering a clotting disorder in which his red blood cells were breaking down faster than the liver could metabolize them. This was the same disorder the scientists had seen in the monkeys that had been given the stronger vector. The condition is life-threatening for anyone, but particularly dangerous for someone with Jesse's disease, because red blood cells liberate protein when they break down.

By midafternoon Tuesday, a little more than 24 hours after the rejection, the clotting disorder had pushed Jesse into a coma. By 11:30 P.M., his ammonia level was 393 micromoles per liter of blood. Normal is 35. The doctors began dialysis. . . .

By Wednesday afternoon, Jesse seemed to be stabilizing. Batshaw went back to Washington. Paul felt comfortable enough to meet his brother for dinner. But later that night Jesse worsened again. His lungs grew stiff; the doctors were giving him 100 percent oxygen, but not enough of it was getting to his bloodstream. They consulted a liver-transplant team and learned that Jesse was not a good candidate. Raper was beside himself. He consulted with Batshaw and Wilson, and they decided to take an extraordinary step, a procedure known as ECMO, for extracorporeal membrane oxygenation, essentially an external lung that filters the blood, removing carbon dioxide and adding oxygen. It had been tried on only 1,000 people before, Raper says. Only half had survived.

"If we could just buy his lungs a day or two," Raper said later, they thought "maybe he would go ahead and heal up.". . .

An Unknown Cause

On the morning of Friday the 17th, a test showed that Jesse was brain dead. Paul Gelsinger didn't need to be told: "I knew it already." He called for a chaplain to hold a bedside service, with prayers for the removal of life support.

The room was crowded with equipment and people: 7 of Paul's 15 siblings came in, plus an array of doctors and nurses. Raper and Batshaw, shellshocked and exhausted, stood in the back. The chaplain anointed Jesse's forehead with oil, then read the Lord's Prayer. The doctors fought back tears. When the intensive-care specialist flipped two toggle switches, one to turn off the ventilator and the other to turn off the ECMO machine, Raper stepped forward. He checked the heart-rate monitor, watched the line go flat and noted the time: 2:30 P.M. He put his stethoscope to Jesse's chest, more out of habit than necessity, and pronounced the death official. "Goodbye, Jesse," he said. "We'll figure this out."

Wilson reported the death immediately, drawing praise from government officials but criticism from Arthur Caplan, who says they should have made the news public, in a news conference. In the weeks since, the Penn team has put every detail of Jesse's treatment under a microscope. It has rechecked the vector to make certain it was not tainted, tested the same lot on monkeys, re-examined lab and autopsy findings. Wilson's biggest fear was that Jesse died as a result of human error, but so far there has been no evidence of that. "That's what's so frightening," French Anderson says. "If they made a mistake, you would feel a little safer."

Remarks by the President on Limiting Stem Cell Research

GEORGE W. BUSH

In a nationally televised address on the evening of August 9, 2001, U.S. president George W. Bush outlined his position on stem cell research, human cloning, and the role of government in regulating these practices. Bush had to address two questions: Would his government allow the cloning of stem cells, and should this research receive federal tax dollars? Bush notes in this address that although studies have suggested that stem cells may hold the secret to the treatment of many diseases, including Alzheimer's and Parkinson's, some people object to the research, arguing that the embryos destroyed in the process of stem cell cultivation are fully human and should be regarded as such under the law. Public opinion on the issue is deeply divided, and the compromise reached by Bush reflects this rift. Based on his decision, scientists are allowed to continue research on existing cell lines drawn from frozen embryos, as well as on adult and animal stem cells, but no federal funds will be given to research that utilizes new donor embryos.

George W. Bush, "Remarks by President George W. Bush on Stem Cell Research," www.whitehouse.gov, August 2001.

The issue of research involving stem cells derived from human embryos is increasingly the subject of a national debate and dinner table discussions. The issue is confronted every day in laboratories as scientists ponder the ethical ramifications of their work. It is agonized over by parents and many couples as they try to have children, or to save children already born.

The issue is debated within the church, with people of different faiths, even many of the same faith coming to different conclusions. Many people are finding that the more they know about stem cell research, the less certain they are about the right ethical and moral conclusions.

The Promise of Stem Cell Research

My administration must decide whether to allow federal funds, your tax dollars, to be used for scientific research on stem cells derived from human embryos. A large number of these embryos already exist. They are the product of a process called in vitro fertilization, which helps so many couples conceive children. When doctors match sperm and egg to create life outside the womb, they usually produce more embryos than are planted in the mother. Once a couple successfully has children, or if they are unsuccessful, the additional embryos remain frozen in laboratories.

Some will not survive during long storage; others are destroyed. A number have been donated to science and used to create privately funded stem cell lines. And a few have been implanted in an adoptive mother and born, and are today healthy children.

Based on preliminary work that has been privately funded, scientists believe further research using stem cells offers great promise that could help improve the lives of those who suffer from many terrible diseases—from juvenile diabetes to Alzheimer's, from Parkinson's to spinal cord injuries. And while scientists admit they are not yet certain, they believe stem cells derived from embryos have unique potential.

You should also know that stem cells can be derived from sources other than embryos—from adult cells, from umbilical cords that are discarded after babies are born, from human placenta. And many scientists feel research on these types of stem cells is also promising. Many patients suffering from a range of diseases are already being helped with treatments developed from adult stem cells.

However, most scientists, at least today, believe that research on embryonic stem cells offer the most promise because these cells have the potential to develop in all of the tissues in the body.

The Greater Good

Scientists further believe that rapid progress in this research will come only with federal funds. Federal dollars help attract the best and brightest scientists. They ensure new discoveries are widely shared at the largest number of research facilities and that the research is directed toward the greatest public good.

The United States has a long and proud record of leading the world toward advances in science and medicine that improve human life. And the United States has a long and proud record of upholding the highest standards of ethics as we expand the limits of science and knowledge. Research on embryonic stem cells raises profound ethical questions, because extracting the stem cell destroys the embryo, and thus destroys its potential for life. Like a snowflake, each of these embryos is unique, with the unique genetic potential of an individual human being.

As I thought through this issue, I kept returning to two fundamental questions: First, are these frozen embryos human life, and therefore, something precious to be protected? And second, if they're going to be destroyed anyway, shouldn't they be used for a greater good, for research that has the potential to save and improve other lives?

I've asked those questions and others of scientists, scholars, bioethicists, religious leaders, doctors, researchers, members of Congress, my Cabinet, and my friends. I have read heartfelt letters from many Americans. I have given this issue a great deal of thought, prayer and considerable reflection. And I have found widespread disagreement.

The Arguments

On the first issue, are these embryos human life—well, one researcher told me he believes this five-day-old cluster of cells is not an embryo, not yet an individual, but a pre-embryo. He argued that it has the potential for life, but it is not a life because it cannot develop on its own.

An ethicist dismissed that as a callous attempt at rationalization. Make no mistake, he told me, that cluster of cells is the same way you and I, and all the rest of us, started our lives. One goes with a heavy heart if we use these, he said, because we are dealing with the seeds of the next generation.

And to the other crucial question, if these are going to be destroyed anyway, why not use them for good purpose—I also found different answers. Many argue those embryos are by-products of a process that helps create life, and we should allow couples to donate them to science so they can be used for good purpose instead of wasting their potential. Others will argue there's no such thing as excess life, and the fact that a living being is going to die does not justify experimenting on it or exploiting it as a natural resource.

Fundamental Questions

At its core, this issue forces us to confront fundamental questions about the beginnings of life and the ends of science. It lies at a difficult moral intersection, juxtaposing the need to protect life in all its phases with the prospect of saving and improving life in all its stages.

As the discoveries of modern science create tremendous hope, they also lay vast ethical mine fields. As the genius of science extends the horizons of what we can do, we increasingly confront complex questions about what we should do. We have arrived at that brave new world that seemed so distant in 1932, when Aldous Huxley wrote about human beings created in test tubes in what he called a "hatchery."

In recent weeks [July 2001], we learned that scientists have created human embryos in test tubes solely to experiment on them. This is deeply troubling, and a warning sign that should prompt all of us to think through these issues very carefully.

Embryonic stem cell research is at the leading edge of a series of moral hazards. The initial stem cell researcher was at first reluctant to begin his research, fearing it might be used for human cloning. Scientists have already cloned a sheep. Researchers are telling us the next step could be to clone human beings to create individual designer stem cells, essentially to grow another you, to be available in case you need another heart or lung or liver.

I strongly oppose human cloning, as do most Americans. We recoil at the idea of growing human beings for spare body parts, or creating life for our convenience. And while we must devote enormous energy to conquering disease, it is equally important that we pay attention to the moral concerns raised by the new frontier of human embryo stem cell research. Even the most noble ends do not justify any means.

My position on these issues is shaped by deeply held beliefs. I'm a strong supporter of science and technology, and believe they have the potential for incredible good—to improve lives, to save life, to conquer disease. Research offers hope that millions of our loved ones may be cured of a disease and rid of their suffering. I have friends whose children suffer from juvenile diabetes. [Former First Lady] Nancy Reagan has written me about President [Ronald] Reagan's struggle with Alzheimer's. My own family has confronted the tragedy of childhood leukemia. And, like all Americans, I have great hope for cures.

I also believe human life is a sacred gift from our Creator.

I worry about a culture that devalues life, and believe as your President I have an important obligation to foster and encourage respect for life in America and throughout the world. And while we're all hopeful about the potential of this research, no one can be certain that the science will live up to the hope it has generated.

Existing Stem Cell Lines

Eight years ago, scientists believed fetal tissue research offered great hope for cures and treatments—yet, the progress to date has not lived up to its initial expectations. Embryonic stem cell research offers both great promise and great peril. So I have decided we must proceed with great care.

As a result of private research, more than 60 genetically diverse stem cell lines already exist. They were created from embryos that have already been destroyed, and they have the ability to regenerate themselves indefinitely, creating ongoing opportunities for research. I have concluded that we should allow federal funds to be used for research on these existing stem cell lines, where the life and death decision has already been made.

Leading scientists tell me research on these 60 lines has great promise that could lead to breakthrough therapies and cures. This allows us to explore the promise and potential of stem cell research without crossing a fundamental moral line, by providing taxpayer funding that would sanction or encourage further destruction of human embryos that have at least the potential for life.

I also believe that great scientific progress can be made through aggressive federal funding of research on umbilical cord, placenta, adult and animal stem cells, which do not involve the same moral dilemma. This year [2001], your government will spend $250 million on this important research.

I will also name a President's council [the President's Council on Bioethics] to monitor stem cell research, to recommend appropriate guidelines and regulations, and to consider all of the medical and ethical ramifications of biomedical innovation. This council will consist of leading scientists, doctors, ethicists, lawyers, theologians and others, and will be chaired by Dr. Leon Kass, a leading biomedical ethicist from the University of Chicago.

This council will keep us apprised of new developments and give our nation a forum to continue to discuss and evaluate these important issues. As we go forward, I hope we will always be guided by both intellect and heart, by both our capabilities and our conscience.

I have made this decision with great care, and I pray it is the right one.

Stem Cell Research Should Continue

GERALD D. FISCHBACH AND RUTH L. FISCHBACH

Because stem cells have the potential to develop into different types of cells, they offer scientists the opportunity to research and potentially treat various medical conditions that are the result of abnormal cell development, such as cancer or birth defects. Stem cells could also be used to produce tissues and organs for transplantation as treatment for a myriad of conditions from heart disease to spinal cord injuries. A third potential application of stem cell research is the treatment of disease through the implantation of stem cells engineered to provide the patient with a healthy genetic makeup, which could be used to treat diabetes or Parkinson's.

When President George W. Bush banned the use of federal funds for the creation of human stem cells in August 2001, he believed that there were already sixty-two stem cell lines in existence and that these would provide adequate material for public research to continue. In the following article Gerald D. Fischbach, dean of the Faculty of Medicine at Columbia University, and Ruth L. Fischbach, director of the Center for Bioethics at Columbia, argue that even if there were sixty-two useable stem cell lines (it turned out that there were fewer than five) the number is insufficient to provide for genetic diversity, thereby limiting scientific research. According to the authors, promising research is being hindered by politics and fundamentalist dogma that misunderstands stem cell biology by wrongly considering an embryo to be equivalent to an individual.

Gerald D. Fischbach and Ruth L. Fischbach, "Stem Cells: Science, Policy, and Ethics," *The Journal of Clinical Investigation*, vol. 114, November 2004, pp. 1,364–70. Copyright © 2004 by *The Journal of Clinical Investigation*. Reproduced by permission of Copyright Clearance Center.

Few subjects in biomedical science have captured the imagination of both the scientific community and the public as has the use of stem cells for the repair of damaged tissues. Because they may be able to replace cells that have atrophied or have been lost entirely, stem cells offer the hope of restoration of cellular function and relief from suffering associated with many disabling disorders. Beyond tissue repair, cultured stem cells might also find application in the analyses of disease mechanisms and normal development, as assays for screening new drugs, and as vehicles for gene therapy.

The Promise of Stem Cell Research

Each potential use of stem cells promises revolutionary advances. However, the word "promise" must be underscored—to date, no cures have been realized, no disease mechanisms have been uncovered, and no new drugs have been developed. Many in the international scientific community believe that the promise of stem cell–based studies or therapies will be realized only if we can derive new human embryonic stem cell (hESC) lines.

At the present time, the production of new cell lines involves destruction of preimplantation embryos at the 100–200 cell (blastocyst) stage. Debate currently centers on the moral status of these embryos, which are now stored at in vitro fertilization (IVF) clinics or created by somatic cell nuclear transfer (SCNT). . . . What is the moral status of the blastocyst? Should blastocysts be protected under the same laws that govern research on human subjects? These and related questions are at the center of a debate that involves the lay public, the scientific community, the press, and the United States Congress. . . .

Current Regulations

In early 2000, Harriet Raab, then General Counsel of the DHHS [Department of Health and Human Services], adopted the view that stem cells are not organisms (embryos) and hence are not covered by 45CFR46 [the regulations that cover research on human subjects] or by the Dickey Amendment [which extended 45CFR46 to include human embryos]. Research on hESCs could, therefore, be supported by government funds, provided that the cells were derived from embryos using private funds. This opinion was adopted by Harold Varmus, then-Director of the NIH [National Institutes of Health] but it caused an uproar in Congress as many members felt that the Raab opinion was a legalism that violated the spirit of the law. Nevertheless, the NIH formed a committee of scientists, lawyers, patient advocates, and clergy to consider guidelines for the use of hESCs. They labored for many months. The final document stated that an NIH grantee could use these hESCs provided several criteria were met, including the following: (a) the stem cells were derived from embryos produced in IVF clinics for reproductive purposes; (b) the stem cells were in excess of clinical need, meaning that the donors had achieved a successful pregnancy or had simply decided not to proceed with IVF; (c) the stem cells were derived from embryos that were frozen, allowing sufficient time between the emotional experience of creating the embryos and the decision regarding donation; (d) informed consent and institutional review board approval was obtained: and (e) no exchange of money was made, in order to avoid a financial influence.

As of March 2004, there were more than 400,000 frozen embryos stored in IVF clinics nationwide. The options open to donors of these embryos are to destroy them, offer them up for adoption, continue to store them, or donate them for medical research.

These NIH guidelines were accepted by President [Bill] Clinton but rejected by President George W. Bush soon thereafter. In his speech of August 9, 2001, President Bush recognized the value of research on hESCs and the promise of successful cell replacement therapies. However, he said that he would not condone the destruction of additional embryos to create new hESC lines. At the time, he believed that 62 hESC lines were available in labs around the world, and he made it clear that all subsequent federally supported research would be confined to these existing lines.

There Are Not Enough Stem Cell Lines

Reaction in the scientific community was mixed. Some were relieved that the President recognized the importance of hESC research. Other investigators, skeptical about the existence of 62 cell lines, were disappointed. In the following months it became obvious that there were not 62 usable cell lines; there were fewer than 5. The number of available lines has since grown, and 21 lines are currently listed in the NIH registry. However, the tangle of intellectual property requirements and the fact that most of these hESC lines were cultured in contact with mouse cells and bovine serum limits their utility. Moreover, many of them still have not been well characterized in terms of viability and their ability to differentiate. . . .

Whether it is 5, 21, or 62, the number of available hESC lines is simply not sufficient to provide for the genetic diversity among the recipient population. In developing a new medicine, one would not stop with the first chemical that produced an effect. Efficacy must be optimized and safety must be taken into account.

Creation of new cell lines from human embryos can proceed thanks to support from nongovernment sources. Recently 17 new hESC lines were derived with private funds, and more are sure to follow. However, in the long run, the talent represented by the community of scientists supported by the NIH and other federal agencies will be needed for this field to move forward.

Currently in the House of Representatives a bill introduced by [Representatives Dave] Weldon . . . and [Bart] Stupak [passed in Feb. 2005] . . . and in the Senate a bill introduced by [Senators Sam] Brownback . . . and [Mary] Landrieu [still undecided] . . . would outlaw the formation of human embryos by SCNT in the private sector as well as by researchers receiving federal funds. This extraordinary legislation would criminalize scientific research, making it punishable by a $1 million fine and 10 years in prison. Effects of this chilling attack on the scientific process extend beyond hESC research. It casts a pall over all science. It indicates a widening gulf between those in public office and the scientific community—a reversal of the coming together of political and scientific minds over the stem cell debate that we are observing in other nations. . . .

Those opposed to research on embryos are concerned that we are on a slippery slope, facing a creeping moral degradation fostered by unbridled biotechnology. If we agree to destroy an organism that has the potential to develop into a human being, it may be easy to move on to other destructive acts. This zeal poses the danger of depriving millions who suffer from degenerative disorders of the hope and benefits that might derive from stem cell–based research.

The Fourteenth Day

There is no absolute right answer to the debate regarding the dissociation of blastocysts to produce more hESC lines. Here we present several considerations that convince us of the ethical validity of using embryos up until the 14th day after fertilization.

Up to embryonic day 14, the blastocyst has no central nervous system and, in our view, cannot be considered sensate. We now remove organs from patients who have been declared brain dead but who are still alive in some sense (e.g., they are warm, breathing, making urine). The use of these organs has saved many lives. We view these two-hundred-cell embryos as cell donors certainly at the same moral status or less than these individuals.

The slippery slope argument that the use of blastocysts created by SCNT will lead to reproductive cloning is not compelling. With appropriate federal regulations and oversight, such as the *Hatch-Feinstein Bill*, introduced in the Senate by Orrin Hatch and Dianne Feinstein [originally rejected, but reintroduced in February 2005], which seeks to prohibit human reproductive cloning while preserving the use of blastocysts to enhance stem cell research, the scientific community can proceed in an orderly fashion. The UK [United Kingdom] is now succeeding in this vein under the watchful eye of its Human Fertilisation and Embryology Authority, a nongovernmental body that regulates and inspects all UK clinics providing IVF, donor insemination, and embryo storage while also licensing and monitoring all human embryo research conducted in the UK. The guidepost—implantation into a uterus—is an unambiguous barrier.

The need for hESC research is extraordinary. We are on the doorstep of a new type of restorative therapy that goes beyond treating disease symptoms. Disorders in which the lesions are focal will be the first to undergo stem cell therapy. Replacing ß cells in the pancreas, motor neurons in the spinal cord, and dopaminergic cells in the basal ganglia are the most obvious examples. We must weigh the obligations of the moral imperative to help suffering individuals against the inherent value of preimplantation blastocysts.

We have many examples in history where attempts to outlaw fields of study have led to terrible and terrifying consequences (from Galileo to Lysenko). Conversely, many technological breakthroughs now highly valued by both the scientific and lay communities, such as IVF or heart transplants, were once thought to be too dangerous or were seen as "playing God".

Finally, this effort should go forward because we simply will not know the answers unless we do the research. The desire to know is absolutely intrinsic to humans and has a survival value as well as a moral one.

The Mapping of the Human Genome Is Completed

FRANCIS S. COLLINS

On April 14, 2003, it was announced that the international effort to sequence the human genome was complete. The following selection was originally given as testimony before the U.S. House of Representatives by the leader of the project, Francis S. Collins, one month later. Focusing on the future of the project and the impact it will have on biology, health, and society, he argues that it "will make a profound difference to the health and well being of all the people of this world." Ultimately, knowledge of the complete genome sequence will allow scientists to develop predictive tests for many conditions, gene-based designer drugs, and, possibly, treatments for cancer. It will also allow for more sophisticated diagnosis and treatment of mental illness, he contends. Collins is the director of the National Human Genome Research Institute.

The main goals of the [Human Genome Project (HGP)] were first articulated in 1988 by a special committee of the U.S. National Academy of Sciences (NAS), and later adopted through a detailed series of five-year plans jointly written by the National Institutes of Health (NIH) and the Department of Energy (DOE). In 1988 Dr. James D. Watson, who won the Nobel Prize along with Francis Crick for discovering the structure of DNA, was appointed to head the

Francis S. Collins, "The Future of Genomics," www.genome.gov, National Human Genome Research Institute, May 22, 2003.

then Office of Human Genome Research, which has grown into the National Human Genome Research Institute [NHGRI] that I now have the privilege of directing. As of April 14, 2003, the principal goals laid out by the NAS have all been achieved more than two years ahead of schedule and $400 million dollars under budget, including the essential completion of a high-quality version of the human sequence. Other goals included the creation of physical and genetic maps of the human genome, which provided a necessary lower resolution view of the genome and have major value to research in their own right. The HGP also accomplished the mapping and sequencing of a set of five model organisms, including the mouse. That information generally empowers the ability to interpret the human genome, rather like the Rosetta stone allowed the decryption of the ancient languages. The NAS study also recommended that, "access to all sequence and materials generated by these publicly funded projects should and even must be made freely available [to all]." We have adhered to that noble standard throughout the last 13 years. . . .

[In April 2003], we were able to observe a major anniversary, the fiftieth anniversary of the discovery of the double helix structure of DNA by Drs. Watson and Crick, while simultaneously celebrating the completion of the DNA sequence of the human genome. In June 2000, the NHGRI and its partners in the International Human Genome Sequencing Consortium had already completed a "working draft" of the human genome sequence; at that same time, Celera Genomics [a private biotechnology company] under Dr. Craig Venter's leadership, released its own draft version of the human genome and participated with us in a joint announcement at the White House. Since then the federally funded sequencing centers and our international partners have been working to correct all the remaining spelling errors and fill in the gaps in the draft sequence, leading to the public release of the essentially complete sequence on April 14, 2003. This is the reference sequence we will be using for all time. The availability of the 3 billion letters of the human instruction book could be said to mark the starting point of the genomic era in biology and medicine. There is now much important work to do to deliver on the promise that these advances in genomics offer for human health. . . .

A New Vision for the Future of Genomics

This April [2003] also witnessed the publication in the journal *Nature* of a bold vision for the future of genomics research, developed by the NHGRI. This vision, the outcome of almost two years of intense discussions with literally hundreds of scientists and members of the public, has three major areas of focus: Genomics to Biology, Genomics to Health, and Genomics to Society.

Genomics to Biology: The human genome sequence provides foundational information that now will allow development of a comprehensive catalog of all of the genome's components, determination of the function of all human genes, and [the] deciphering of how genes and proteins work together in pathways and networks.

Genomics to Health: Completion of the human genome sequence offers a unique opportunity to understand the role of genetic factors in health and disease, and to apply that understanding rapidly to prevention, diagnosis, and treatment. This opportunity will be realized through such genomics-based approaches as identification of genes and pathways and determining how they interact with environmental factors in health and disease, more precise prediction of disease susceptibility and drug response, early detection of illness, and development of entirely new therapeutic approaches.

Genomics to Society: Just as the HGP has spawned new areas of research in basic biology and in health, it has created new opportunities in exploring the ethical, legal, and social implications (ELSI) of such work. These include defining policy options regarding the use of genomic information in both medical and non-medical settings and analysis of the impact of genomics on such concepts as race, ethnicity, kinship, individual and group identity, health, disease, and "normality" for traits and behaviors.

This vision for the future of genomics is not just about the NHGRI. It encompasses the whole field of genomics, including the work of all the other Institutes and Centers at the NIH and of a number of other federal agencies. All of the NIH Institutes are already taking full advantage of the sequence and will apply its data to the better understanding of both rare and common diseases, almost all of which have a genetic component. A recent example of the way that the HGP and the knowledge and new technologies it has spawned are already facilitating science is the extremely rapid sequencing by groups in Canada and at the Centers for Disease Control and Prevention (CDC) in Atlanta of the genome of the virus that causes Severe Acute Respiratory Syndrome (SARS). The sequencing of the SARS virus genome provides insight into this new and deadly disease at a speed never before possible in science. In turn, this should lead to the rapid development of diagnostic tests and, in time, vaccines and effective treatments.

New Initiatives

The NHGRI has already begun several new initiatives, and is planning others, to meet the challenge of realizing this new vision for the future of genomics. Many of these initiatives will be co-funded by other NIH Institutes, other federal and international partners, and the private sector. Some examples of these cutting edge programs include:

The Creation of a Human Haplotype Map: Multiple genetic and environmental factors influence many common diseases, such as diabetes, cancer, stroke, mental illness, heart disease, and arthritis; however, relatively little is known about the details of the genetic basis of such common diseases. Together with international partners, the NHGRI has begun to create a "haplotype map" of the human genome to enable scientists to find the genes that affect common diseases more quickly and efficiently. The power of this map stems from the fact that each DNA variation is not inherited independently; rather, sets of variations tend to be inherited in blocks. The specific pattern of particular genetic variations in a block is called a "haplotype." This new initiative, an international public/private partnership led and managed by NHGRI, will develop a catalog of haplotype blocks, the "HapMap." The HapMap will provide a new tool to identify genetic variations associated with disease risk or response to environmental factors, drugs, or vaccines. It will allow more efficient genomic research and clinical applications, thus making for more economical use of research and health care funds. Ultimately, this powerful tool will lead to more complete understanding of, and improved treatments for, many common diseases.

The ENCODE Project: the ENCyclopedia Of DNA Elements: To utilize fully the information that the human genome sequence contains, a comprehensive encyclopedia of all of its functional elements is needed. The identity and precise location of all transcribed sequences, including both protein-coding and non-protein coding genes, must be determined. The identity of other functional elements encoded in the DNA sequence, including signals that determine whether a gene is "on" or "off", and determinants of chromosome structure and function, also is needed. The NHGRI has developed a public research consortium to carry out a pilot project, focusing on a carefully chosen set of regions of the human genome, to compare existing and new methods for identifying functional genetic elements. This ENCyclopedia Of DNA Elements (ENCODE) consortium, which welcomes all academic, government, and private sector scientists interested in facilitating the comprehensive interpretation of the human genome, will greatly enhance use of the human genome sequence to understand the genetic basis of human health and to stimulate the development of new therapies to prevent and treat disease.

Genome Technology Development: The NHGRI continues

to invest in technology development that speeds the applications of genomics. Technical advances have caused the cost of DNA sequencing to decline dramatically, from $10 in 1990 to less than $0.09 per base pair in 2002, but this cost must decline even further for all to benefit from genomic advances. The NHGRI, along with many partners, will actively pursue the development of new technologies to sequence any individual's genome for $1,000 or less. Other areas of technology development are also ripe for expansion, and the NHGRI plans to pursue them vigorously.

A Vision of the Future of Genomic Medicine

While it always is somewhat risky to predict the future, I want to leave you with my view of where I believe genomic medicine is headed. In the next ten years, I expect that predictive genetic tests will exist for many common conditions in which interventions can alleviate inherited risk, so that each of us can learn of our individual risks for future illness and practice more effective health maintenance and disease prevention. By the year 2020, gene-based designer drugs are likely to be available for conditions like diabetes, Alzheimer's disease, hypertension, and many other disorders. Cancer treatment will precisely target the molecular fingerprints of particular tumors, genetic information will be used routinely to give patients more appropriate drug therapy, and the diagnosis and treatment of mental illness will be transformed.

[The year 2003] marks a very exciting transition in the field of genomics, with the full sequencing of the human genome marking the successful achievement of all of the HGP's original goals, and thus the advent of the genomic era. When Congress decided to fund the HGP, it did so with the justifiable belief that this work would lead to improved health for all. Those advances are already occurring all around us, and the ability to accelerate the realization of this vision now lies before us. At the same time, we must be sure that these technological advances can benefit all our citizens in a safe and appropriate manner. It is our sincere belief that the newly created discipline of genomics will make a profound difference to the health and well being of all the people of this world.

While I am very optimistic about the future of genomic medicine, we clearly have a great deal more work to do to realize these lofty goals. The vision for the future of genomic medicine that I have described will require major breakthroughs in technology and scientific knowledge. But I am confident that by supporting our best and brightest scientists to work together with our partners within the government and around the globe, we will meet these challenges.

Designer Babies Are on the Way

SHANNON BROWNLEE

In October 2001 the world's first genetically engineered primate was born in the Oregon Regional Primate Research Center. Named ANDi, the rhesus monkey was engineered to carry a gene that makes jellyfish glow in the dark. Although ANDi failed to express the inserted gene (he did not glow), he nonetheless made headlines, leading many to speculate about the increased possibility of genetically engineering humans. Shannon Brownlee, freelance biotechnology journalist and senior fellow at the New America Foundation, reports that the genetic modification of humans had already begun some years before ANDi's birth in private fertility clinics, which are largely unregulated. In fact, she claims, the only thing currently stopping fertility clinics from producing "made-to-order" children is the ethics of individual fertility specialists and the sizable technical hurdles that complicate the procedure. According to Brownlee, the uncontrolled experimentation on humans currently under way not only poses serious health risks for its subjects but may also have a profound and unforeseeable effect on the human gene pool.

In the mid-1990s, embryologist Jacques Cohen pioneered a promising new technique for helping infertile women have children. His technique, known as cytoplasmic transfer, was intended to "rescue" the eggs of infertile women who had undergone repeated, unsuccessful attempts at in vitro fertilization, or IVF. It involved injecting the cytoplasm found inside the eggs of a fertile donor, into the patient's eggs.

When the first baby conceived through cytoplasmic transfer was born in 1997, the press instantly hailed Cohen's technique as yet another technological miracle. But four years later, the real story has proven somewhat more complicated. Last year [2001] Cohen and his colleagues at the Institute for Reproductive Medicine and Science of St. Barnabas, a New Jersey fertility clinic, set off alarm bells among bioethicists with the publication of a paper detailing the genetic condition of two of the 17 cytoplasmic-transfer babies born through the clinic to date. The embryologists reported that they had endowed the children with extra bits of a special type of genetic material, known as mitochondrial DNA, or mtDNA, which came with the cytoplasm transferred from the donor eggs to the patient's.

That meant the resulting children had three genetic parents: mother, father, and mtDNA donor. It also meant that female children would transmit their unorthodox combination of mitochondrial DNA to their own offspring (mtDNA is passed down only through eggs), with unknown implications. In effect, Cohen had created the first bioengineered babies. As Cohen's group noted, their experiment was "the first case of human [inheritable] genetic modification resulting in normal, healthy children."

"A Step into the Dark"

Just how normal those children will turn out to be is anybody's guess. At a recent meeting in Europe, the New Jersey researchers reported that one of the children conceived through cytoplasmic transfer has been diagnosed with "pervasive developmental disorder," a catch-all term for symptoms that range from mild delays in speech to autism. Cohen's group maintained that it is extremely unlikely that cytoplasmic transfer and the resulting mishmash of mtDNA is to blame.

But geneticists have only begun to trace the connections between mtDNA and a host of diseases ranging from strange metabolic ailments to diabetes and Lou Gehrig's disease, and some experts argued that the child's disorder may well be caused by a mismatch between the donor and mother's mtDNA. As Jim Cummins, a molecular biologist at Murdoch University in Western Australia, put it: "To deliberately create individuals with multiple mitochondrial genotypes without knowing the consequences is really a step into the dark."

Welcome to the murky world of "reprogenetics," as Princeton biologist Lee Silver has dubbed the merger between the science of genetics and the fertility industry. While much of the nation's attention has been focused on human cloning, a possibility that is still largely theoretical, a massive, uncontrolled experiment in bioengineering humans is well underway in the Wild West of American fertility clinics, as Cohen and his colleagues have demonstrated. Indeed, there has been more debate over—and far more research into—the implications of bioengineered corn than of bioengineered humans.

Made-to-Order Children

Now, many bioethicists believe that Cohen's experiment with cytoplasmic transfer was just one more small step towards a world in which eugenics is another name for making babies. Today, any couple with several thousand dollars to spare can choose the sex of their offspring, while parents who are carriers for certain genetic disorders can undergo IVF and have the resulting embryos genetically tested to ensure their children are free of disease. Tomorrow, parents may be able to enhance their offspring with designer genes. One day, the fertility industry's efforts to help couples conceive could bring society to the brink of altering the genetic heritage of the species.

All that currently stands in the way of parents bent on practicing homegrown eugenics are the ethics of individual fertility specialists and the technical hurdles. Most fertility doctors have the best of intentions, to help patients get pregnant, and to avoid transmitting debilitating disease. And it is by no means certain that science will ever be able to offer parents the option of bioengineering their offspring.

All the same, the pace of the technology is dizzying. A year ago [in October 2001], scientists at the Oregon Regional Primate Research Center announced the birth of the first genetically engineered primate, named ANDi (for "inserted DNA" spelled backwards), a rhesus monkey whose cells contained the gene that makes jellyfish glow in the dark. The experiment was something of a flop: ANDi does not glow. (Rodents implanted with the gene do.) But imagine that one day science does acquire the skills to make "designer babies," that the connections between genes and complex traits such as intelligence or musical ability are finally known. While only the weirdest of parents would want to genetically engineer offspring with jellyfish genes, others would undoubtedly jump at the chance to "customize" their children with a sparkling personality, brains, and beauty.

One need not be deeply religious or oppose abortion to be troubled by the prospect of a society in which, as bioethicist Alexander Capron puts it, "the wanted child becomes the made-to-order child."

A Biological Product

One near-term possibility [is] that many parents, if given the opportunity, will want to weed out embryos carrying genetic traits for a host of non-lethal conditions, like baldness, shyness, short stature, or homosexuality. Fertility specialists are already getting requests from prospective parents who want to know if they can be assured their embryos won't turn out to be hyperactive or gay. Today, Tom Sawyer and Huck Finn would have been diagnosed with attention-deficit disorder and medicated. Tomorrow, they might not be allowed out of the petri dish.

Yet thanks largely to abortion politics and our collective squeamishness about intruding on the individual's right to become a parent, the nation has few mechanisms in place for controlling the pace of this new technology, ensuring the safety of patients, or even talking about the ethics of such experiments.

Since 1998, the Food and Drug Administration (FDA) has argued that genetically manipulated embryos are a "biological product," and therefore subject to regulation, just like medical devices and drugs. But because of a quirk in federal law, the FDA's authority in this sphere is far from certain.

Last summer [2001], FDA sent warning letters to six fertility centers threatening "enforcement action," and asserting its regulatory power over "therapy involving the transfer of genetic material by means other than the union of [sperm and egg.]" Cohen's clinic at St. Barnabas chose to stop performing cytoplasmic transfer. But at least two other recipients scoffed at the agency's threat: Panos Zavos, an embryologist at a Kentucky fertility clinic, and Brigitte Boisselier, the scientific director of Clonaid, the clinic set up by a group known as the Raelians, who believes human beings were genetically engineered by aliens. Both have announced their intentions to clone a human being.

Both also disputed the FDA's authority, and several bioethicists and legal scholars had to agree that the FDA could not prevent them from tinkering with human bioengineering. "It's a stretch for the FDA," says R. Alta Charo, a legal scholar and bioethicist at the University of Wisconsin, and former member of President Bill Clinton's Bioethics Advisory Committee. . . .

Unknown Dangers

The industry trade group, the American Society for Reproductive Medicine [ASRM], argues that fertility doctors are doing nothing different from any other specialist. "Reproductive medicine starts from the same regulatory basis as every other kind of medicine," says ASRM spokesman, Sean Tipton. If a heart surgeon thinks a new way of tying off an artery might work, she simply does it. If the patient

lives, she tries it again. Eventually, she n
spective look at her cases and compare tl
those who received the new method versus

It is also true, however, that the history o
littered with examples of doctors unquestion
ing new treatments long before they have beer.   ⌐,
only to abandon them when they turn out to ⌐⌐ ineffec-
tive—or worse. More than 30,000 women with breast cancer received high dose chemotherapy with bone-marrow
transplants in the 1980s and 90s. At least 9,000 died from
the treatment before researchers finally performed clinical
trials, which ultimately demonstrated that high dosage is
no better than standard chemotherapy regimens.

The deeper question, of course, is why we allow uncontrolled experimentation on human subjects in any branch
of medicine. But the issue is particularly pressing for reproductive technologies, especially now that fertility centers
are wading into the uncharted waters of the gene pool.

Embryologists have already experimented with transferring the nucleus of an older woman's egg into a young
donor's egg from which the nucleus has been removed, a
technique that is similar to the method used to create Dolly,
the [cloned] sheep. Another fertility team successfully split
a human embryo into several identical copies, a trick that
could one day help infertile women who produce very few
eggs. But it could also make possible such . . . scenarios as
multiple identical embryos being thawed and then born
several years apart, or a woman giving birth to herself.

Baby Blues

In hindsight, perhaps the anti-abortion activists who
feared the emergence of technology like IVF were right to
step back and question the larger implications. While few
Americans would begrudge infertile couples the babies
that have been produced through IVF, the issues now being raised by genetic engineering are not ones to be
taken lightly, and a national consensus can only be ar-

at through vigorous public debate.

Some of that debate emerged in 2000, when Lisa and Jack Nash briefly made the news when their son Adam was born in Colorado. The Nashes already had one child, six-year-old Molly, who was born with a rare genetic bone marrow disease that would kill her unless she received a transplant from someone with the identical tissue type. Both Lisa and Jack were carriers for Fanconi anemia, a genetic disorder leaving them with a one-in-four chance of having another affected child each time Lisa got pregnant.

The Nashes elected, instead, to conceive 15 embryos and subject them to PGD, or pre-implantation genetic diagnosis. A single cell was taken from each embryo and tested for the presence of the genetic mutation that causes Fanconi anemia. Then the Nashes went a step further, and had the embryos checked to see which one carried a tissue type that matched their daughter, Molly's. Adam was born in Denver in August. In September, doctors in Minnesota performed a stem cell transplant on Molly, using blood taken at birth from Adam's umbilical cord and his bone marrow. Today, the Nashes have two healthy children. Faced with the same situation, many American parents would undoubtedly choose the same course.

At the same time, the Nash case raises the unsettling possibility of parents bearing children not to love and cherish them, but for the purpose of harvesting their tissue. And what about parents who simply want their kids to be like them, genetic warts and all? Consider the deaf lesbian couple in Washington, D.C., who recently sought a sperm donor who was also congenitally deaf, so they could be assured of a deaf child. Such desires might seem reasonable if not for the fact that any parent who deafened a hearing baby would be charged with child abuse.

The "Standard of Care"

Under the current political landscape, the nation has little control over what it deems acceptable. Americans may one day decide that it is perfectly all right to genetically engineer children with blue skin or webbed feet or any other trait that parents see fit. In the meantime, current practices in the fertility industry could use some oversight. Thus far, however, the only legislative response to worrisome reproductive technologies has been to ban them and accuse their practitioners of "playing God," an argument that appeals to conservative constituents but will in the short term, at least, prove futile. Says former bioethics committee member Charo, "As soon as you have absolute prohibitions you run into constitutional challenges."

Over the long term, banning certain technologies, such as reproductive cloning, may well be advisable, but reining in the pace of reprogenetics now is going to take a network of regulatory solutions. First on the list: Update the FDA's decades-old charter. In recent years, Congress has generally sided with business against the agency, beating back its efforts to rein in the herbal medicine industry for example. But legislators have already signaled their distaste for reproductive cloning, and the balance of power is likely to shift when it comes to giving the FDA regulatory control over reprogenetics.

The FDA, along with the U.S. Department of Health and Human Services (HHS), jointly oversee the protection of human subjects in clinical trials, which are required to demonstrate safety and efficacy before new drugs or medical devices can be licensed for market. Most of the time, companies put their products through rigorous testing in animals long before proceeding to human experimentation. Applying the same standards to human embryo experiments would compel fertility clinics to perform similar tests before subjecting patients to new reprogenetic technologies. It would also entail the creation of specialized review boards with the expertise to evaluate human reproductive experiments.

Tweaking tort law would also impose greater discipline on fertility doctors and would-be human genetic engineers.

Current malpractice law rests on the idea of negligence, which means that plaintiffs must demonstrate that a doctor failed to provide care in accordance with acceptable standards. In fast-moving, innovative arenas of medicine, such as fertility, there is no established or accepted "standard of care." Not surprisingly, fertility patients almost never sue, in part because they can't find lawyers to take their cases.

One solution, says Charo, is to stop using negligence as the standard for reproductive medicine, and impose strict liability instead. If the patient or child suffers a bad outcome, the clinic is liable, and patients could, in effect, sue for wrongful life.

Oversight of Human Experimentation

England also offers a model for creating boundaries for thornier issues bordering on eugenics. A decade after the birth of the first test-tube baby, Parliament created a licensing board, the Human Fertilization and Embryology Authority (HFEA), which has kept a tight lid on burgeoning genetic technologies since 1991—to the dismay of some would-be patients and clinic directors.

In a recent case before the HFEA, for example, a family with four boys that had lost their young daughter in a fire asked to be allowed to choose female embryos for IVF. HFEA refused, fearing that sex selection for purposes other than to prevent a sex-linked disease, such as hemophilia, would push British society toward eugenics, or at least widespread sex-selection. A national licensing board like the HFEA would probably prove unworkable in this country, but the U.S. would do well to create an advisory panel for reproductive technologies that would provide a public forum for what are now individual decisions with huge social consequences.

Finally, anti-abortion activists need to recognize that federal involvement in embryo research is critical for limiting the risks posed by genetic engineering of the future and improving the current outcomes for families desperately seeking to have a child. Tens of thousands of embryos are discarded by fertility clinics each year because embryologists are not allowed to work on them using federal dollars. If conservatives wish to ban the creation of embryos for the purpose of research, they should focus their formidable political power on allowing research on embryos created in the hopes of producing a child.

Funding such science would certainly bring a higher level of rigor to the field and increased oversight of human experimentation. The nation is already sliding down a slippery slope toward the age of reprogenetics. Our only hope of slowing the pace is to apply the brakes of regulation.

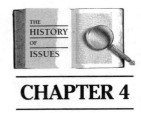

CHAPTER 4

Cloning

Chapter Preface

O f all the debates raised by genetic engineering, none has provoked as strong a response as human cloning. The debate began in 1978 with the publication of David Rorvik's *In His Image: The Cloning of a Man*, an account of a secret human cloning experiment. Although it turned out to be a hoax, the account fooled both scientists and laymen, and provoked strong responses in scientific journals and prominent newspapers. For the next two decades, human cloning returned to the realm of science fiction. This changed on February 1997, when Scottish embryologist Ian Wilmut announced that a sheep cloned from fully differentiated adult cells had been born. Dolly proved that human cloning was a technical possibility, which reignited the cloning debate.

Although a majority of Americans are against human cloning, the nuances and complexities of human cloning technologies ensures that the controversy remains difficult to resolve. One of the major disputes in this debate is a matter of definition. While some lump all human cloning into one category, others argue that human cloning can take two distinct forms. The first is reproductive cloning, which results in the birth of an individual whose genetic makeup is identical to that of an already existing person. For this to occur, a cloned embryo must be implanted into a woman's womb and carried to term. The second type is therapeutic cloning, which results in a cloned human embryo. In this type of cloning, however, the embryo is not implanted and does not result in the birth of a baby.

Advocates of reproductive cloning argue that there is nothing inherently unethical about cloning and that cloning would provide infertile couples with the opportunity to have their own children. They argue that infertility is a disability, and that attempts to ban reproductive cloning are, according to patient advocate Mark Eibert, "violations of the constitutional right to have children." Opponents feel that the dangers that reproductive cloning pose outweigh the reproductive rights of couples. For example, the clone is likely to experience physical defects, as so many cloned animals do. The clone may also feel a loss of identity or uniqueness. Many critics believe that cloning humans amounts to playing God.

Although most Americans are against reproductive cloning, a majority is for therapeutic cloning used in embryonic stem cell research. Therapeutic cloning advocates argue that the embryos created in the lab are nothing more than a microscopic collection of cells, not a human being, and so destroying them in the course of research does not constitute killing. Advocates also argue that the medical breakthroughs promised by therapeutic cloning research outweigh all other ethical considerations. The possible benefits of this research include the creation of replacement organs matched to the genetic makeup of the patient, the production of stem cells that could be used to replace damaged tissues, and the advancement of scientific knowledge about inheritable diseases. In contrast, therapeutic cloning opponents argue that therapeutic cloning is unethical. Pope John Paul II argued that "these techniques, insofar as they involve the manipulation and destruction of human embryos, are not morally acceptable, even when their proposed goal is good in itself." For these critics human life begins at conception, and the creation and subsequent destruction of embryos is morally unacceptable.

During Rorvik's time it was perhaps easy to dismiss human cloning as nothing more than science fiction. Today, as advances in genetic engineering seem to occur almost daily, and with therapeutic cloning experimentation underway, the prospect of human clones walking the earth seems less far-fetched.

Cloning and the Future of Human Evolution

JOSHUA LEDERBERG

*In September 1966 Nobel laureate Joshua Lederberg pub-
lished an astonishing article in the* American Naturalist, *in
which he speculated about the future of human cloning. Scientists had only just successfully cloned tadpoles for the first
time a few years before, and Lederberg was already proph-
esying the cloning of humans. By examining the biology of
plants, Lederberg concluded that the ideal evolutionary strategy for any species is a mix of both sexual and clonal reproduction. He was suggesting, for the first time, that humankind
might be able to improve itself by manipulating reproduction,
linking cloning with the controversial field of eugenics. He
then considered some of the social effects that cloning might
have, the most profound of which would be a new definition
of what it means to be human. Lederberg was a professor of
genetics and served as president of the Rockefeller University
from 1978 to 1990.*

M an is . . . on the brink of a major evolutionary perturbation, but this is not algeny [the attempt to genetically "perfect" a species] but *vegetative propagation*. . . .

For the sake of argument, suppose we could mimic with
human cells what we know in bacteria, the useful transfer
of DNA extracted from one cell line to the chromosomes of

another cell. Suppose we could even go one step further and sprinkle some specified changes of genotype over that DNA. What use could we make of this technology in the production as opposed to the experimental phase? . . .

The Advantages of Clonal Reproduction

Vegetative reproduction, once we are reminded that it is an indispensable facet of experimental technique in the microbial analogy, cannot be . . . readily dismissed. In fact there is ample precedent for it, and not only throughout the plant and microbial kingdoms, but in many lower animals. Monozygotic [identical] twins in man are accidental examples. Experimentally, we know of successful nuclear transplantation from diploid somatic as well as germline cells into enucleated amphibian eggs. There is nothing to suggest any particular difficulty about accomplishing this in mammals or man, though it will rightly be admired as a technical tour-de-force when it is first implemented (or will this sentence be an anachronism before it is published?) Indeed I am more puzzled by the rigor with which apogamous reproduction [the development of an embryo without fertilization] has been excluded from the vertebrate as compared to the plant world, where its short-run advantages are widely exercised. If the restriction is accidental from the standpoint of cell biology, nevertheless a phylum that was able to fall into this trap might be greatly impeded in its evolutionary experimentation towards creative innovation.

Vegetative or clonal reproduction has a certain interest as an investigative tool in human biology, and as an indispensable basis for any systematic algenics; but other arguments suggest that there will be little delay between demonstration and use. Clonality outweighs algeny at a much earlier stage of scientific sophistication, primarily because it answers the technical specifications of the eugenicists in a way that Mendelian [i.e., natural] breeding does not. If a superior individual (and presumably then genotype) is identified, why not copy it directly, rather than suffer all the risks of recombinational disruption, including those of sex. The same solace is accorded the carrier of genetic disease: why not be sure of an exact copy of yourself rather than risk a homozygous segregant; or at worst copy your spouse and allow some degree of biological parenthood. Parental disappointment in their recombinant offspring is rather more prevalent than overt disease. Less grandiose is the assurance of sex-control; nuclear transplantation is the one method now verified.

Indeed, horticultural practice verifies that a mix of sexual and clonal reproduction makes good sense for genetic design. Leave sexual reproduction for experimental purposes; when a suitable type is ascertained, take care to maintain it by clonal propagation. The Plant Patent Act already gives legal recognition to the process, and the rights of the developer are advertised "Asexual Reproduction Forbidden."

The Social Effects of Cloning

Clonality will be available to and have significant consequences from acts of individual decision . . . given only community acquiescence or indifference to its practice. But here this simply allows the exercise of a minority attitude, possibly long before its implications for the whole community can be understood. Most of us pretend to abhor the narcissistic motives that would impel a clonist, but he (or she) will pass just that predisposing genotype intact to the clone. Wherever and for whatever motives close endogamy has prevailed before, clonism and clonishness will prevail.

Apogamy as a way of life in the plant world is well understood as an evolutionary cul-de-sac, often associated with hybrid luxuriance. It can be an unexcelled means of multiplying a rigidly well-adapted genotype to fill a stationary niche. So long as the environment remains static, the members of the clone might congratulate themselves that they had outwitted the genetic load; and they have indeed won a short-term advantage. In the human context, it is at least debatable whether sufficient latent variability to allow for any future contingency were preserved if the population were distributed among some millions of clones. From a strictly biological standpoint, tempered clonality could allow the best of both worlds—we would at least enjoy being able to observe the experiment of discovering whether a second Einstein would outdo the first one. How to temper the process and the accompanying social frictions is another problem.

The internal properties of the clone open up new possibilities, e.g., the free exchange of organ transplants with no concern for graft rejection. More uniquely human is the diversity of brains. How much of the difficulty of intimate communication between one human and another, despite the function of common learned language, arises from the discrepancy in their genetically determined neurological hardware? Monozygotic twins are notoriously sympathetic, easily able to interpret one another's minimal gestures and brief words; I know, however, of no objective studies of their economy of communication. For further argument, I will assume that genetic identity confers neurological similarity, and that this eases communication. This has never been systematically exploited as between twins, though it might be singularly useful in stressed occupations—say a pair of astronauts, or a deep-sea diver and his pump-tender, or a surgical team. It would be relatively more important in the discourse between generations, where an older clonont would teach his infant copy. A systematic division of intellectual labor would allow efficient communicants to have something useful to say to one another.

The burden of this argument is that the cultural process poses contradictory requirements of uniformity (for communication) and heterogeneity (for innovation). We have no idea where we stand on this scale. At least in certain areas—say soldiery—it is almost certain that clones would have a self-contained advantage, partly independent of, partly accentuated by the special characteristics of the genotype which is replicated. This introverted and potentially narrow-minded advantage of a clonish group may be the chief threat to a pluralistically dedicated species.

Experiments in Cloning

Even when nuclear transplantation has succeeded in the mouse, there would remain formidable restraints on the way to human application, and one might even doubt the further investment of experimental effort. However several lines are likely to become active. Animal husbandry, for prize cattle and racehorses, could not ignore the opportunity, just as it bore the brunt of the enterprises of artificial insemination and oval transplantation. The dormant storage of human germ plasm as sperm will be replaced by the freezing of somatic tissues to save potential donor nuclei. Experiments on the efficacy of human nuclear transplantation will continue on a somatic basis, and these tissue clones used progressively in chimeras. Human nuclei, and individual chromosomes and genes of the karyotype [chromosomal pattern], will also be recombined with cells of other animal species—these experiments now well under way in cell culture. Before long we are bound to hear of tests of the effect of dosage of the human 21st chromosome on the development of the brain of the mouse or the gorilla. Extracorporeal gestation would merely accelerate these experiments. As bizarre as they seem, they are direct translations to man of classical work in experimental cytogenetics [the study of heredity] in Drosophila [a small fruit fly] and in many plants. They need no further advance in algeny, just a small step in cell biology.

My colleagues differ widely in their reaction to the idea that anyone could conscientiously risk the crucial experiment, the first attempt to clone a man. Perhaps this will not be attempted until gestation can be monitored closely to be sure the fetus meets expectations. The mingling of individual human chromosomes with other mammals assures a gradualistic enlargement of the field and lowers the threshold of optimism or arrogance, particularly if cloning in other mammals gives incompletely predictable results. What are the practical aims of this discussion? It might help to redirect energies now wasted on naive eugenics and to protect the community from a misapplication of genetic policy. It may sensitize students to recognize the significance of the fruition of experiments like nuclear transplantation. Most important, it may help to provoke more critical use of the lessons of history for the direction of our future. This will need a much wider participation in these concerns. It is hard enough to approach verifiable truth in experimental work; surely much wider criticism is needed for speculations whose scientific verifiability falls in inverse proportion to their human relevance. Scientists are by no means the best qualified architects of social policy, but there are two functions no one can do for them: the apprehension and interpretation of technical challenges to expose them for political action, and forethought for the balance of scientific effort that may be needed to manage such challenges. Popular trends in scientific work towards effective responses to human needs move just as slowly as other social institutions, and good work will come only from a widespread identification of scientists with these needs.

The foundations of any policy must rest on some deliberation of purpose. One test that may appeal to skeptical scientists is to ask what they admire in the trend of human history. Few will leave out the growing richness of man's inquiry about nature, about himself and his purpose. As long as we insist that this inquiry remain open, we have a pragmatic basis for a humble appreciation of the value of innumerable different approaches to life and its questions, of respect for the dignity of human life and of individuality, and we decry the arrogance that insists on an irrevocable answer to any of these questions of value. The same humility will keep open the options for human nature until their consequences to the legacy momentarily entrusted to us are fully understood. These concerns are entirely consistent with the rigorously mechanistic formulation of life which has been the systematic basis of recent progress in biological science.

A New Definition of "Human"

Humanistic culture rests on a definition of man which we already know to be biologically vulnerable. Nevertheless the goals of our culture rest on a credo of the sanctity of human individuality. But how do we assay for *man* to demarcate him from his isolated or scrambled tissues and organs, on one side, from experimental karyotypic hybrids on another. Pragmatically, the legal privileges of humanity will remain with objects that look enough like men to grip their consciences, and whose nurture does not cost too much. Rather than superficial appearance of face or chromosomes, a more rational criterion of human identity might be the potential for communication with the species, which is the foundation on which the unique glory of man is built.

Recent discussions of controlled human evolution have focussed on two techniques: selective breeding (eugenics) and genetic alchemy (algeny). The implementation will doubtless proceed even without an adequate basis of understanding of human values, not to mention vast gaps in human genetics.

Eugenics is relatively inefficacious since its reasonable aims are a necessarily slow shift in the population frequencies of favorable genes. Segregation and recombination vitiate most short-range utilities. Its proponents are therefore led to advocate not only individual attention to but the widespread adoption of its techniques, and a minority of them would seek the sanction of law to enforce the doctrine. Most geneticists would insist on a deeper knowledge of human genetics before considering statutory intrusion on personal liberties in this sphere. Meanwhile there is grave danger that the minority view will lead to a confusion of the economic and social aims of rational population policy with genocide. The defensive reaction to such a confusion could be a disastrous impediment to the adoption of family planning by just those groups whose economic and educational progress most urgently demands it.

Algeny presupposes a number of scientific advances that have yet to be perfected; and its immediate application to human biology is, probably unrealistically, discounted as purely speculative. In this paper, I infer that the path to algeny already opens up two major diversions of human evolution: clonal reproduction and introgression of genetic material from other species. Indeed, the essential features of these techniques have already been demonstrated in vertebrates, namely nuclear transplantation in amphibia, and somatic hybridization of a variety of cells in culture, including human.

The Future of Cloning

Paradoxically, the issue of "subhuman" hybrids may arise first, just because of the touchiness of experimentation on obviously human material. Tissue and organ cultures and transplants are already in wide experimental or therapeutic use, but there would be widespread inhibitions about risky experiments leading to an object that could be labelled as a human or parahuman infant. However, there is enormous scientific interest in organisms whose karyotype is augmented by fragments of the human chromosome set, especially as we know so little in detail of man's biological and genetic homology with other primates. This is being and will be pushed in steps as far as biology will allow, to larger and larger proportions of human genome in intact animals, and to organ combinations and chimeras with varying proportions of human, subhuman, and hybrid tissue (note actual efforts to transplant primate organs to man). The hybridization is likely to be somatic, and the elaboration of these steps to make full use of nuclear transplantation to test how well these assorted genotypes will support the full development of a zygote.

Other techniques may well be discovered as shortcuts, especially how to induce the differentiation of a competent egg from somatic tissue, bypassing meiosis. This process has no experimental foundation at present, but plenty of precedent in natural history.

These are not the most congenial subjects for friendly conversation, especially if the conversants mistake comment for advocacy. If I differ from the consensus of my colleagues it may be only in suggesting a time scale of a few years rather than decades. Indeed, we will then face two risks, (1) that our scientific position is extremely unbalanced from the standpoint of its human impact, and (2) that precedents affecting the long-term rationale of social policy will be set, not on the basis of well-debated principles, but on the accidents of the first advertised examples. The accidentals might be as capricious as the nationality, batting average, or public esteem of a clonont, the handsomeness of a parahuman progeny, the private morality of the experimenters, or public awareness that man is part of the continuum of life.

Claims That the First Human Has Been Cloned

DAVID M. RORVIK

In 1978 David M. Rorvik, a respected science writer who had worked for both Time *and the* New York Times, *made the startling claim that the world's first human clone had been born. His book,* In His Image: The Cloning of a Man, *detailed Rorvik's participation in a human cloning project and became the source of international controversy. The book even provoked a congressional hearing. In the ensuing years after the book's publication, Rorvik declined to provide any proof of the claim, and in 1981 a court declared the book to be a "fraud and a hoax."*

The events outlined in the book begin with Rorvik being approached in 1973 by an anonymous American millionaire who wanted Rorvik to use his scientific connections to manage a research project, the aim of which was to produce a clone of the unmarried millionaire. The project would take place in a lab located on an undisclosed island where, according to the book, a surrogate mother gave birth to the man's clone in December 1976. The book brought the issue of human cloning into the public arena for the first time and drew attention to the ethical issues raised by the advances being achieved in the biological sciences. In this excerpt from Rorvik's work, he contemplates the consequences of his participation in the project.

David M. Rorvik, *In His Image: The Cloning of a Man.* London: Hamish Hamilton, 1978. Copyright © 1978 by David M. Rorvik. Reproduced by permission of the publisher.

I have said that I was, if anything, somewhat favourably disposed towards the prospect of human cloning, provided adequate safeguards existed and all due precautions against identifiable areas of abuse were exercised. But that had all been in theory and on paper. I could not now approach the issue in so academic and remote a fashion. A man, whom one might reasonably assume to be on the level, was actually asking me to act as a go-between, a courier in a million-dollar plan that could culminate in what the Nobel Prize–winning geneticist Joshua Lederberg had once described as 'a major evolutionary perturbation'.

Could I afford to be guilty of or party to a perturbation? The word struck me as intrinsically disturbing, its four syllables encompassing the potential for seemingly infinite disorder.

The Impact of a Cloned Human

Some writers had envisaged human cloning as the metaphor of a new age, one in which man literally remakes himself, recreates himself this time in his own image; others as the signpost at the gates of a brave new world in which natural evolution is no more and the new era of 'participatory evolution' reigns supreme. There were, I knew, in the rapidly-unfolding world of molecular biology, both promises far grander and potential perils far blacker than those of human cloning. But their meaning, I realized, was almost hopelessly disguised to the public by the inaccessible code of recondite biochemical equations and abstract recombinant possibilities. Cloning, on the other hand, would, it seemed to me, if suddenly thrust upon the world as a *fait accompli*, stand out like a cosmic sore thumb, signalling for some 'the end' and for others 'the beginning'. Either way it would cause a major commotion.

This might be bad. Mankind, in my view, was already and increasingly beset by a sense of rootlessness and unreality, proceeding in part from its incremental remove from the natural air-earth-water bases of life, to the synthetic, prepackaged, media-manipulated illusions of substance that were all part of the new fading dream of 'Progress' and 'The Good Life'. To some weary time-travellers, cloning might be a heavy blow—heralding the irreversible approach, if not the actual realization, of the synthesized, plasticized, carbon-copied Man. To these, the new man, like the new bread—processed, refined, bleached, artificially preserved and fortified, baked to absolute uniformity and confined in a plastic skin—would be soulless.

And even if I regarded such despair as misplaced I still had to reckon with its impact, try to gauge how deep it might cut, how the spirit of man, already sagging, might decline further under its weight. Even if I regarded as shallow the beliefs of those who would see in clonal man a threat to God's place in the scheme of things, I could not count myself human and disregard the *feelings* of those thus shaken in their faith.

A Biological Backlash

In addition, I had to confront the possibility that a cloned man might create a biological backlash that would be felt for decades, possibly centuries. Cloning, though in itself novel and fascinating, would have to be accounted trivial in comparison with other developments contemplated by serious and humane scientists in the realm of molecular biology—developments that might not only make man healthier but, ultimately, cleverer, better, kinder. There seemed no limit to what might be possible in the wake of a stunning series of breakthroughs that had begun with the decoding of the basic chemical molecules of life. If cloning were to so startle and offend the world, all those glittering hopes of genetic science might be dashed or at least substantially set back to the detriment of millions.

And last, but not least, I had to think about myself, what my involvement in such an undertaking, whether successful or not, would do to my reputation, what it might portend for my own future, and the future of those associated with me. I might, it seemed quite likely, be regarded by some as anything but a high-minded idealist who had helped husband a new era. Some might say I had merely pimped and pandered for it, acted as a mercenary go-between, the uncaring croupier in a round of genetic roulette, the dropper, or at least the polisher, of the die in a game of chromosomal craps. It was unpleasant to think about.

And since my caller had hinted that he had no intention of proceeding in the public eye, and since, moreover, I felt that no one capable of accomplishing this would dare brave the recriminations of his peers by proceeding above board, I knew that I would, if my part in this came to light, be accused of undermining the traditional scientific ethics of full disclosure I held dear. That would be bad, the more so since I would be guilty. On the other hand, if *I* sought to disclose some of the details but was compromised by the need to protect and conceal my sources, out of respect for journalistic ethics I held equally sacred, I might be doubted, disbelieved, even decried as a fraud. That might be worse.

Still, that 'sore thumb' might, on balance, do more good than harm. If technology could be a demon, it could also be a tonic and a restorative. To many, our first, faltering steps into outer space were proof that man's ingenuity and pioneering spirit had not only survived decades of industrial dulling but had prevailed to express themselves in exciting new ways. Some no doubt felt that, in going to the moon and then looking ambitiously beyond that first icy foothold in the once 'unknowable' and forbidding ether, man had overstepped himself, violated nature and perhaps even challenged God. But more of us, I believed, were lifted by these events, encouraged, if anything, to feel more unified, not only with one another but with the universe itself.

The Creation of a Public Debate

In my view an even more exciting and significant adventure was in store for man on the newly opening frontier of biological inner space. The means were at hand, at last, to launch an exploration into the universe within. The cloning of a man, because its impact would be so immediately dramatic, could make this new adventure accessible to millions who might otherwise understand little of what was transpiring in the molecular world.

It was conceivable, then, that the cloning of a man might not inhibit but actually speed up the important research that was poised, like a rocket on a launching pad, ready to go forward. And if the reaction to what Lederberg had called a 'technical tour de force', the cloning of a human being, were to be greeted with mixed reactions, as seemed likely, then one could still argue that this accomplishment had served to focus attention on a field of science which was of the utmost importance to the 'average man' but which was, until now, largely unknown to him. Like a red flag, cloning could alert the world to the awesome possibilities that loomed ahead and thus serve as a catalyst for public participation in the life-and-death decisions that might otherwise be left, by default, to the scientists—men and women who laboured, for the most part, in the interests of humanity but who could not be expected to be all-knowing and all-wise.

In that light, my role in all this might be, it seemed to me, more kindly perceived. I could argue that through my participation there was hope that these events would be disclosed in some form to the public, that, in short, this exercise would have as its ends, at least from my point of view, something more worthy than the mere secret satisfaction of a single individual. There was a certain amount of ego involved in this argument, I knew, for I would be saying that it was lucky for mankind that I, rather than someone less interested in seeing the public interest served, was involved in this. Still, I found the thought of myself playing as much a watch dog as a promoter or procurer attractive. At least, it made it easier for me to contemplate playing a role in this. It was easy to imagine: If I do not do this somebody else will, probably somebody only in it for the money.

The Dangers of Cloning

The idea of all this was still too tentative, too ethereal to make other considerations that would later weigh heavily upon me, yet compelling: what would happen if my caller turned out to be a very clever madman spawning a diabolical power plot? What would happen if something went wrong and this man and his doctors—my God, *we*—created some sort of monster, misshapen in body, mind or both? What happened if the product of eventual 'success' could not adjust to the uniqueness, the utter strangeness of his being? What if, through carelessness in my effort to apprise the public of some of what had happened, I revealed the identity of this unique individual, exposing him to what I had no doubt would be the relentless scrutiny of the rest of the world?

During those three days I experienced all manner of emotions. It was difficult to keep all this to myself. At times I felt like laughing out loud, telling acquaintances about the crazy fellow who had phoned me. The trouble was he did not *seem* crazy while I was talking to him. And I realized, in any event, that I was at least partly responsible for him making this proposal. After all, some of my own writings had contributed to his conviction that human cloning was possible and under some circumstances desirable. Was I now going to try to laugh off what I had written, as if the world of books and articles was all make-believe?

Human Reproductive Cloning Should Be Banned

LEON R. KASS

Leon R. Kass began his career as a molecular biologist but moved from practice to theory when, in 1967, he read an article by Joshua Lederberg that discussed the advantages of human cloning. Kass was so disturbed by the "amoral treatment of this morally weighty subject" that he penned a letter in response and instantly became a main participant in the debate about human cloning. He is a founding member of the bioethics think tank the Hastings Center, a professor at the University of Chicago, and chairman of the President's Council on Bioethics.

In the following selection from 1997, Kass argues that the feeling of repugnance felt by many toward the idea of human reproductive cloning—the creation of babies using cloning technology—is not a simplistic emotion that ought to be overcome by reason but rather a "deeper wisdom" that should be heeded. He asserts that human reproductive cloning must be banned, or any number of biological "perversions," from the depersonalization of procreation to the genetic control of one generation over the next, will result.

"**O**ffensive." "Grotesque." "Revolting." "Repugnant." "Repulsive." These are the words most commonly heard regarding the prospect of human cloning. Such reactions come both from the man or woman in the street and from the intellectuals, from believers and atheists, from humanists and scientists. Even Dolly's creator has said he "would find it offensive" to clone a human being.[1]

The Wisdom of Repugnance

People are repelled by many aspects of human cloning. They recoil from the prospect of mass production of human beings, with large clones of look-alikes, compromised in their individuality; the idea of father-son or mother-daughter twins; the bizarre prospects of a woman giving birth to and rearing a genetic copy of herself, her spouse or even her deceased father or mother; the grotesqueness of conceiving a child as an exact replacement for another who has died; the utilitarian creation of embryonic genetic duplicates of oneself, to be frozen away or created when necessary, in case of need for homologous tissues or organs for transplantation; the narcissism of those who would clone themselves and the arrogance of others who think they know who deserves to be cloned or which genotype any child-to-be should be thrilled to receive; the Frankensteinian hubris to create human life and increasingly to control its destiny; man playing God. Almost no one finds any of the suggested reasons for human cloning compelling; almost everyone anticipates its possible misuses and abuses. Moreover, many people feel oppressed by the sense that there is probably nothing we can do to prevent it from happening. This makes the prospect all the more revolting.

Revulsion is not an argument; and some of yesterday's repugnances are today calmly accepted—though, one must add, not always for the better. In crucial cases, how-

1. Dolly the sheep was the first mammal cloned from an adult. Her birth was announced February 22, 1997, and meant that human cloning had become a technical possibility.

ever, repugnance is the emotional expression of deep wisdom, beyond reason's power fully to articulate it. Can anyone really give an argument fully adequate to the horror which is father-daughter incest (even with consent), or having sex with animals, or mutilating a corpse, or eating human flesh, or even just (just!) raping or murdering another human being? Would anybody's failure to give full rational justification for his or her revulsion at these practices make that revulsion ethically suspect? Not at all. On the contrary, we are suspicious of those who think that they can rationalize away our horror, say, by trying to explain the enormity of incest with arguments only about the genetic risks of inbreeding.

The repugnance at human cloning belongs in this category. We are repelled by the prospect of cloning human beings not because of the strangeness or novelty of the undertaking, but because we intuit and feel, immediately and without argument, the violation of things that we rightfully hold dear. Repugnance, here as elsewhere, revolts against the excesses of human willfulness, warning us not to transgress what is unspeakably profound. Indeed, in this age in which everything is held to be permissible so long as it is freely done, in which our given human nature no longer commands respect, in which our bodies are regarded as mere instruments of our autonomous rational wills, repugnance may be the only voice left that speaks up to defend the central core of our humanity. Shallow are the souls that have forgotten how to shudder.

The goods protected by repugnance are generally overlooked by our customary ways of approaching all new biomedical technologies. The way we evaluate cloning ethically will in fact be shaped by how we characterize it descriptively, by the context into which we place it, and by the perspective from which we view it. The first task for ethics is proper description. And here is where our failure begins.

Typically, cloning is discussed in one or more of three familiar contexts, which one might call the technological, the liberal and the meliorist. Under the first, cloning will be seen as an extension of existing techniques for assisting reproduction and determining the genetic makeup of children. Like them, cloning is to be regarded as a neutral technique, with no inherent meaning or goodness, but subject to multiple uses, some good, some bad. The morality of cloning thus depends absolutely on the goodness or badness of the motives and intentions of the cloners: as one bioethicist defender of cloning puts it, "the ethics must be judged [only] by the way the parents nurture and rear their resulting child and whether they bestow the same love and affection on a child brought into existence by a technique of assisted reproduction as they would on a child born in the usual way."

The liberal (or libertarian or liberationist) perspective sets cloning in the context of rights, freedoms and personal empowerment. Cloning is just a new option for exercising an individual's right to reproduce or to have the kind of child that he or she wants. Alternatively, cloning enhances our liberation (especially women's liberation) from the confines of nature, the vagaries of chance, or the necessity for sexual mating. Indeed, it liberates women from the need for men altogether, for the process requires only eggs, nuclei and (for the time being) uteri—plus, of course, a healthy dose of our (allegedly "masculine") manipulative science that likes to do all these things to mother nature and nature's mothers. For those who hold this outlook, the only moral restraints on cloning are adequately informed consent and the avoidance of bodily harm. If no one is cloned without her consent, and if the clonant is not physically damaged, then the liberal conditions for licit, hence moral, conduct are met. Worries that go beyond violating the will or maiming the body are dismissed as "symbolic"—which is to say, unreal.

The meliorist perspective embraces valetudinarians and also eugenicists. The latter were formerly more vocal in these discussions, but they are now generally happy to see their goals advanced under the less threatening banners of freedom and technological growth. These people see in cloning a new prospect for improving human beings—minimally, by ensuring the perpetuation of healthy individuals by avoiding the risks of genetic disease inherent in the lottery of sex, and maximally, by producing "optimum babies," preserving outstanding genetic material, and (with the help of soon-to-come techniques for precise genetic engineering) enhancing inborn human capacities on many fronts. Here the morality of cloning as a means is justified solely by the excellence of the end, that is, by the outstanding traits of individuals cloned—beauty, or brawn, or brains. . . .

The Profundity of Sex

Sexual reproduction—by which I mean the generation of new life from (exactly) two complementary elements, one female, one male, (usually) through coitus—is established (if that is the right term) not by human decision, culture or tradition, but by nature; it is the natural way of all mammalian reproduction. By nature, each child has two complementary biological progenitors. Each child thus stems from and unites exactly two lineages. In natural generation, moreover, the precise genetic constitution of the resulting offspring is determined by a combination of nature and chance, not by human design: each human child shares the common natural human species genotype, each child is genetically (equally) kin to each (both) parent(s), yet each child is also genetically unique.

These biological truths about our origins foretell deep truths about our identity and about our human condition altogether. Every one of us is at once equally human, equally enmeshed in a particular familial nexus of origin, and equally individuated in our trajectory from birth to death—and, if all goes well, equally capable (despite our mortality) of participating, with a complementary other, in the very same renewal of such human possibility through procreation. Though less momentous than our common humanity, our genetic individuality is not humanly trivial.

It shows itself forth in our distinctive appearance through which we are everywhere recognized; it is revealed in our "signature" marks of fingerprints and our self-recognizing immune system; it symbolizes and foreshadows exactly the unique, never-to-be-repeated character of each human life.

Human societies virtually everywhere have structured child-rearing responsibilities and systems of identity and relationship on the bases of these deep natural facts of begetting. The mysterious yet ubiquitous "love of one's own" is everywhere culturally exploited, to make sure that children are not just produced but well cared for and to create for everyone clear ties of meaning, belonging and obligation. But it is wrong to treat such naturally rooted social practices as mere cultural constructs (like left- or right-driving, or like burying or cremating the dead) that we can alter with little human cost. What would kinship be without its clear natural grounding? And what would identity be without kinship? We must resist those who have begun to refer to sexual reproduction as the "traditional method of reproduction," who would have us regard as merely traditional, and by implication arbitrary, what is in truth not only natural but most certainly profound. . . .

The Perversity of Cloning

Cloning creates serious issues of identity and individuality. The cloned person may experience concerns about his distinctive identity not only because he will be in genotype and appearance identical to another human being, but, in this case, because he may also be twin to the person who is his "father" or "mother"—if one can still call them that. What would be the psychic burdens of being the "child" or "parent" of your twin? The cloned individual, moreover, will be saddled with a genotype that has already lived. He will not be fully a surprise to the world. People are likely always to compare his performances in life with that of his alter ego. True, his nurture and his circumstance in life will be different; genotype is not exactly destiny. Still, one must also expect parental and other efforts to shape this new life after the original—or at least to view the child with the original version always firmly in mind. Why else did they clone from the star basketball player, mathematician and beauty queen—or even dear old dad—in the first place?

Since the birth of Dolly, there has been a fair amount of doublespeak on this matter of genetic identity. Experts have rushed in to reassure the public that the clone would in no way be the same person, or have any confusions about his or her identity: as previously noted, they are pleased to point out that the clone of Mel Gibson would not be Mel Gibson. Fair enough. But one is shortchanging the truth by emphasizing the additional importance of the intrauterine environment, rearing and social setting: genotype obviously matters plenty. That, after all, is the only reason to clone, whether human beings or sheep. The odds that clones of Wilt Chamberlain will play in the NBA are, I submit, infinitely greater than they are for clones of [short economist] Robert Reich.

Curiously, this conclusion is supported, inadvertently, by the one ethical sticking point insisted on by friends of cloning: no cloning without the donor's consent. Though an orthodox liberal objection, it is in fact quite puzzling when it comes from people (such as [bioethicist] Ruth Macklin) who also insist that genotype is not identity or individuality, and who deny that a child could reasonably complain about being made a genetic copy. If the clone of Mel Gibson would not be Mel Gibson, why should Mel Gibson have grounds to object that someone had been made his clone? We already allow researchers to use blood and tissue samples for research purposes of no benefit to their sources: my falling hair, my expectorations, my urine and even my biopsied tissues are "not me" and not mine. Courts have held that the profit gained from uses to which scientists put my discarded tissues do not legally belong to me. Why, then, no cloning without consent—including, I assume, no cloning from the body of someone who just died? What harm is done the donor, if genotype is "not me"? Truth to tell, the only powerful justification for objecting is that genotype really does have something to do with identity, and everybody knows it. If not, on what basis could Michael Jordan object that someone cloned "him," say, from cells taken from a "lost" scraped-off piece of his skin? The insistence on donor consent unwittingly reveals the problem of identity in all cloning. . . .

Therapy vs. Enhancement

We do . . . already practice negative eugenic selection, through genetic screening and prenatal diagnosis. Yet our practices are governed by a norm of health. We seek to prevent the birth of children who suffer from known (serious) genetic diseases. When and if gene therapy becomes possible, such diseases could then be treated, in utero or even before implantation—I have no ethical objection in principle to such a practice (though I have some practical worries), precisely because it serves the medical goal of healing existing individuals. But therapy, to be therapy, implies not only an existing "patient." It also implies a norm of health. In this respect, even germline gene "therapy," though practiced not on a human being but on egg and sperm, is less radical than cloning, which is in no way therapeutic. But once one blurs the distinction between health promotion and genetic enhancement, between so-called negative and positive eugenics, one opens the door to all future eugenic designs. "To make sure that a child will be healthy and have good chances in life": this is [law professor John] Robertson's principle, and owing to its latter clause it is an utterly elastic principle, with no boundaries. Being over eight feet tall will likely produce some very good chances in life, and so will having the looks of Marilyn Monroe, and so will a genius-level intelligence.

Proponents want us to believe that there are legitimate uses of cloning that can be distinguished from illegitimate uses, but by their own principles no such limits can be found. (Nor could any such limits be enforced in practice.) Reproductive freedom, as they understand it, is governed solely by the subjective wishes of the parents-to-be (plus the avoidance of bodily harm to the child). The sentimentally appealing case of the childless married couple is, on these grounds, indistinguishable from the case of an individual (married or not) who would like to clone someone famous or talented, living or dead. Further, the principle here endorsed justifies not only cloning but, indeed, all future artificial attempts to create (manufacture) "perfect" babies.

A concrete example will show how, in practice no less than in principle, the so-called innocent case will merge with, or even turn into, the more troubling ones. In practice, the eager parents-to-be will necessarily be subject to the tyranny of expertise. Consider an infertile married couple, she lacking eggs or he lacking sperm, that wants a child of their (genetic) own, and propose to clone either husband or wife. The scientist-physician (who is also co-owner of the cloning company) points out the likely difficulties—a cloned child is not really their (genetic) child, but the child of only *one* of them; this imbalance may produce strains on the marriage; the child might suffer identity confusion; there is a risk of perpetuating the cause of sterility; and so on—and he also points out the advantages of choosing a donor nucleus. Far better than a child of their own would be a child of their own choosing. Touting his own expertise in selecting healthy and talented donors, the doctor presents the couple with his latest catalog containing the pictures, the health records and the accomplishments of his stable of cloning donors, samples of whose tissues are in his deep freeze. Why not, dearly beloved, a more perfect baby?

Ban Human Cloning Now

The "perfect baby," of course, is the project not of the infertility doctors, but of the eugenic scientists and their supporters. For them, the paramount right is not the so-called right to reproduce but what biologist Bentley Glass called, a quarter of a century ago, "the right of every child to be born with a sound physical and mental constitution, based on a sound genotype . . . the inalienable right to a sound heritage." But to secure this right, and to achieve the requisite quality control over new human life, human conception and gestation will need to be brought fully into the bright light of the laboratory, beneath which it can be fertilized, nourished, pruned, weeded, watched, inspected, prodded, pinched, cajoled, injected, tested, rated, graded, approved, stamped, wrapped, sealed and delivered. There is no other way to produce the perfect baby.

Yet we are urged by proponents of cloning to forget about the science fiction scenarios of laboratory manufacture and multiple-copied clones, and to focus only on the homely cases of infertile couples exercising their reproductive rights. But why, if the single cases are so innocent, should multiplying their performance be so off-putting? (Similarly, why do others object to people making money off this practice, if the practice itself is perfectly acceptable?) When we follow the sound ethical principle of universalizing our choice—"would it be right if everyone cloned a Wilt Chamberlain (with his consent, of course)? Would it be right if everyone decided to practice asexual reproduction?"—we discover what is wrong with these seemingly innocent cases. The so-called science fiction cases make vivid the meaning of what looks to us, mistakenly, to be benign.

Though I recognize certain continuities between cloning and, say, in vitro fertilization, I believe that cloning differs in essential and important ways. Yet those who disagree should be reminded that the "continuity" argument cuts both ways. Sometimes we establish bad precedents, and discover that they were bad only when we follow their inexorable logic to places we never meant to go. Can the defenders of cloning show us today how, on their principles, we will be able to see producing babies ("perfect babies") entirely in the laboratory or exercising full control over their genotypes (including so-called enhancement) as ethically different, in any essential way, from present forms of assisted reproduction? Or are they willing to admit, despite their attachment to the principle of continuity, that the complete obliteration of "mother" or "father," the complete depersonalization of procreation, the complete manufacture of human beings and the complete genetic control of one generation over the next would be ethically problematic and essentially different from current forms of assisted reproduction? If so, where and how will they draw the line, and why? I draw it at cloning, for all the reasons given.

Therapeutic Cloning Should Be Banned

RICHARD M. DOERFLINGER

In the summer of 2001 the U.S. House of Representatives debated the introduction of two competing bills that addressed the issue of human cloning. The first, known as H.R. 1644, or "The Human Cloning Prohibition Act of 2001," sought to ban all forms of human cloning. The second, H.R. 2172, "The Cloning Prohibition Act of 2001," would allow for therapeutic cloning, or the creation of cloned human embryos for medical applications, but would criminalize reproductive cloning, the implanting of those embryos into a surrogate mother for the purposes of reproduction.

In the following statement, prepared by Richard M. Doerflinger, deputy director of the Secretariat for Pro-Life Activities for the U.S. Conference of Catholic Bishops, four arguments are offered for the adoption of H.R. 1644 and the rejection of H.R. 2172. One is that all human cloning constitutes reproductive cloning, as the creation of a live embryo is by definition the first step of reproduction. Two, therapeutic cloning would pave the way for future reproductive cloning. Three, there are viable alternatives to embryonic stem cell research, such as using adult stem cells. Finally, cloned embryos would be subjected to treatment considered unacceptable if performed on natural human embryos.

H.R. 1644 passed the House of Representatives on July 31, 2001, by a vote of 265 to 162. However, divisions in the Senate prevented the proposal from passing into law. There are

---

Richard M. Doerflinger, prepared statement before the U.S. House Subcommittee on Health, Committee on Energy and Commerce, Washington, DC, July 2001.

currently no laws in the United States that ban cloning completely, although current regulations prohibit federal funding for human cloning research.

The sanctity and dignity of human life is a cornerstone of Catholic moral and social teaching. We believe a society can be judged by the respect it shows for human life, especially in its most vulnerable stages and conditions. At first glance, human cloning may not seem to threaten respect for life because it is presented as a means for creating life, not destroying it. Yet it shows disrespect for life in the very act of generating it. Here human life does not arise from an act of love, but is manufactured in the laboratory to preset specifications determined by the desires of others. Developing human beings are treated as objects, not as individuals with their own identity and rights. Because cloning completely divorces human reproduction from the context of a loving union between man and woman, such children have no "parents" in the usual sense. As a group of experts advising the Holy See has written:

> In the cloning process the basic relationships of the human person are perverted: filiation, consanguinity, kinship, parenthood. A woman can be the twin sister of her mother, lack a biological father and be the daughter of her grandmother. In vitro fertilization has already led to the confusion of parentage, but cloning will mean the radical rupture of these bonds.

From the dehumanizing nature of this technique flow many disturbing consequences. Because human clones would be produced by a means that involves no loving relationship, no personal investment or responsibility for a new life, but only laboratory technique, they would be uniquely at risk of being treated as "second-class" human beings.

In the present state of science, attempts to produce a liveborn child by cloning would require taking a callous attitude toward human life. Animal trials show that 95 to 99% of cloned embryos die. Of those which survive, many are stillborn or die shortly after birth. The rest may face unpredictable but potentially devastating health problems. Those problems are not detectable before birth, because they do not come from genetic defects as such—they arise from the disorganized expression of genes, because cloning plays havoc with the usual process of genetic reorganization in the embryo.

Scenarios often cited as *justifications* for human cloning are actually *symptoms* of the disordered view of human life that it reflects and promotes. It is said that cloning could be used to create "copies" of illustrious people, or to replace a deceased loved one, or even to provide genetically matched tissues or organs for the person whose genetic material was used for the procedure. Each such proposal is indicative of a utilitarian view of human life, in which a fellow human is treated as a means to someone else's ends—instead of as a person with his or her own inherent dignity. This same attitude lies at the root of human slavery.

Let me be perfectly clear. In objective reality a cloned human being would not be an "object" or a substandard human being. Whatever the circumstances of his or her origin, he or she would deserve to be treated as a human person with an individual identity. But the depersonalized technique of manufacture known as cloning disregards this dignity and sets the stage for further exploitation. Cloning is not wrong because cloned human beings would lack human dignity—it is wrong because they *have* human dignity, and are being brought into the world in a way that fails to respect that dignity.

Ironically, startling evidence of the dehumanizing aspects of cloning is found in some proposals ostensibly aimed at *preventing* human cloning. These initiatives would not ban human cloning at all—but would simply ban any effort to allow cloned human embryos to survive. In these proposals, researchers are allowed to use cloning for the unlimited mass production of human embryos for experimentation—and are then required by law to destroy them, instead of allowing them to implant in a woman's womb.

The Cloning Prohibition Act of 2001

In other words: Faced with a 99% death rate from cloning, such proposals would "solve" the problem by ensuring that the death rate rises to 100%. No live clones, therefore no evidence that anyone performed cloning. This is reassuring for researchers and biotechnology companies who may wish the freedom to make countless identical human guinea pigs for lethal experiments. It is no great comfort to the dead human clones; nor is it a solution worthy of us as a nation.

[Republican] Congressman [Jim] Greenwood's "Cloning Prohibition Act of 2001" (H.R. 2172) is even worse than previous bills of this kind. It would actually have the Department of Health and Human Services authorize and *license* the practice of destructive cloning.[1] In a new way, our government would be actively involved in human cloning—but only to ensure that no cloned embryos get out of the laboratory alive. Under the guise of a ban on cloning, the government would assist researchers in refining their procedure; then, ten years after the date of enactment, it would obligingly drop all penalties for using cloning to initiate a pregnancy, so they could use their newly honed skills to manufacture babies. This bill would even invalidate any future state law seeking to establish a genuine ban on cloning, by preempting any such law that does not take the same irresponsible approach.

Sometimes it is said that such proposals would ban "reproductive cloning" or "live birth cloning," while allowing "therapeutic cloning" or "embryo cloning." This may sound superficially reasonable. If banning all cloning is too difficult a task, perhaps we could ban half of it—and the half

1. The bill did not pass.

that is "therapeutic" sounds like the half we'd like to keep.

But this description relies on a fundamental confusion as to what cloning is. I can sum up the real situation in a few propositions.

Embryo Cloning

All human cloning is embryo cloning. Some accounts of cloning seem to imagine that cloning for research purposes produces an embryo, while cloning for reproductive purposes produces a baby or even a fully grown adult—like new copies of Michael Keaton or Arnold Schwarzenegger springing full-grown from a laboratory. This is, of course, nonsense. In the words of Professor Lee Silver of Princeton University, a leading advocate of human cloning: "Real biological cloning can only take place at the level of the cell."

Cloning technology can also be used to produce other kinds of cells; these are not the subject of this hearing, and they are explicitly excluded from the scope of Congressman [Dave] Weldon's legislation [that is, H.R. 1644]. But when somatic cell nuclear transfer is used to replace the nucleus of an egg with the nucleus of a human body cell and the resulting cell is stimulated, a human embryo results, whatever one's ultimate plans on what to do next.

Reproductive Cloning

In an important sense, all human cloning is reproductive cloning. Once one creates a live human embryo by cloning, one has engaged in reproduction—albeit a very strange form of asexual reproduction. All subsequent stages of development—gestation, birth, infancy, etc.—are simply those which normally occur in the development of any human being (though reaching them may be far more precarious for the cloned human, due to the damage inflicted by the cloning procedure).

To say this is not to make a controversial moral claim about personhood or legal rights. It is to state a biological fact: Once one produces an embryo by cloning, a new living being has arrived and the key event in reproduction has taken place. The complete human genome that once belonged to one member of the human species now also belongs to another. Anything that now happens to this being will be "environmental" influence upon a being already in existence—transfer to a womb and live birth, for example, are chiefly simple changes in location.

Moreover, even government study commissions favoring harmful human embryo experiments concede that with the generation of a new embryo, a new life has come into the world. They describe the early embryo as "a developing form of human life" which "warrants serious moral consideration."

Thus generating this new human life in the laboratory confronts us with new moral questions: Not "Should we clone?" but "What do we do with this living human we have produced by cloning?" If all the available answers are lethal to the cloned human 95% to 100% of the time, we should not allow cloning.

"Therapeutic" Cloning

All human cloning, at present, is experimental cloning. The line between "reproductive" and "experimental" cloning is especially porous at present, because any attempt to move toward bringing a cloned child to live birth would first require many thousands of trials using embryos *not* intended for live birth. Years of destructive research of this kind may be necessary before anyone could bring a cloned human through the entire gestational process with any reasonable expectation of a healthy child. Therefore legislation which seeks to bar creation of a cloned embryo for purposes of live birth, while allowing unlimited experimental cloning, would actually facilitate efforts to refine the cloning procedure and prepare for the production of liveborn children. This would be irresponsible in light of the compelling principled objections to producing liveborn humans by cloning.

No human cloning is "therapeutic" cloning. The attempt

to label cloning for purposes of destructive experiments as "therapeutic cloning" is a stroke of marketing genius by supporters of human embryo research. But it does serious damage to the English language and common sense, for two reasons.

First, the experiments contemplated here are universally called "nontherapeutic experimentation" in law and medical ethics—that is, the experiments harm or kill the research subject (in this case the cloned human embryo) without any prospect of benefitting that subject. This standard meaning of "nontherapeutic" research is found, for example, in various state laws forbidding such research on human embryos as a crime. Experiments performed on one subject solely for possible benefit *to others* are never called "therapeutic research" in any other context, and there is no reason to change that in this context.

Second, the "therapeutic" need for human cloning has always been highly speculative; it now seems more doubtful than ever in light of recent advances in adult stem cell research and other noncontroversial alternatives. In the stem cell research debate, as [A. Zitner in the April 27, 2001, *Los Angeles Times*] observes, "There is one thing everyone agrees on: Adult stem cells are proving to be far more versatile than originally thought." Adult stem cells have shown they can be "pluripotent"—producing a wide array of different cells and tissues. They can also be multiplied in culture to produce an ample supply of tissue for transplantation. Best of all, using a patient's own cells solves all problems of tissue rejection, the chief advantage cited until now for use of cloning.

Adult Stem Cells

In 1997 the National Bioethics Advisory Commission reviewed the idea of cloning human embryos to create "customized stem cell lines" but described this as "a rather expensive and far-fetched scenario"—and added that a moral assessment is necessary as well:

Because of ethical and moral concerns raised by the use of embryos for research purposes it would be far more desirable to explore the direct use of human cells of adult origin to produce specialized cells or tissues for transplantation into patients.

Now PPL Therapeutics, the Scottish firm involved in creating "Dolly" the [cloned] sheep, says it has indeed found a way to reprogram ordinary adult cells to become stem cells capable of being directed to form almost any kind of cell or tissue—without creating or destroying any embryos.

Even in the field of embryonic stem cell research, new developments have called into question the need for cloning. The problem of tissue rejection may not be as serious as once thought when cells from early human development are used, and there are other ways of solving the problem—for example, by genetically modifying cells to become a closer match to a patient.

Morally Abhorrent

For all these reasons, a recent overview of the field [by P. Aldhous, in the April 5, 2001, issue of *Nature*] concludes that human "therapeutic cloning" is "falling from favour," that "many experts do not now expect therapeutic cloning to have a large clinical impact." Even James Thomson of the University of Wisconsin, a leading practitioner and advocate of embryonic stem cell research generally, calls this approach "astronomically expensive"; in light of the enormous wastefulness of the cloning process and the damage it does to gene expression, "many researchers have come to doubt whether therapeutic cloning will ever be efficient enough to be commercially viable" even if one could set aside the grave moral issues involved.

We should clearly understand what would be entailed by any effort to implement a "therapeutic cloning" regimen for stem cell transplants. This would not be a case in which human embryos are destroyed once to form a permanent cell line for future use. For *each individual patient*, countless human embryos—the patient's genetic twin brothers or sisters—would have to be created in the laboratory and then destroyed for their stem cells, in the hope of producing genetically matched tissue for transplantation. Thus the creation and destruction of human life in the laboratory would become an ongoing aspect not only of medical research but of everyday medical practice. And what would become of those who have profound moral objections to cloning, and to having new lives created and destroyed for our benefit? Would we be told that we must choose between our life and our conscience?

In short, the "therapeutic" case for cloning is as morally abhorrent as it is medically questionable. Which brings me to a final proposition on how to assess proposals for preventing human cloning.

A Cloned Embryo Is Human

Because cloned humans are humans, any proposal to prevent human cloning must not do to cloned humans anything that would be universally condemned if done to other humans at the same stage of development.

This proposition can be universally endorsed by people on both sides of the cloning issue, and on both sides of the abortion issue. To quote Lee Silver once more: "Cloned children will be full-fledged human beings, indistinguishable in biological terms from all other members of the human species." Thus, for example, cloned embryos deserve as much respect as other human embryos of the same stage—whatever that level of respect may be.

Silver's point about cloned humans being "indistinguishable" from others raises a major practical problem for efforts to allow creation of cloned embryos while forbidding their transfer to a womb. Once the embryo is created in a fertility clinic's research lab (as such a law would permit) and is available for transfer, *how could the government tell* that this embryo was or was not created by cloning? And if it cannot do so, how can it enforce a prohibition on transferring cloned embryos (but not IVF [in vitro fertilization] embryos) to a woman's womb?

Mandated Murder

However, an even more serious moral and legal issue arises at this point. If the government allows use of cloning to produce human embryos for research but prohibits initiating a pregnancy, what will it be *requiring* people to do? If pregnancy has already begun, the only remedy would seem to be government-mandated abortion—or at least, jailing or otherwise punishing women for remaining pregnant and giving birth. We need not dwell on the abhorrence such a solution would rightly provoke among people on all sides of the abortion issue. It would be as "anti-choice" as it is "anti-life."

However, even if the law could act before transfer actually occurs, the problem is equally intractable. For the law would have to *require* that these embryos be killed—defining for the first time in U.S. history a class of human embryos that it is a crime *not* to destroy. It is impossible to reconcile such a law with the profound "respect" and "serious moral consideration" that even supporters of human embryo research say should be accorded to all human embryos.

If the law *permitted* (or, even worse, *licensed*) creation of cloned embryos for research, while prohibiting their creation for any other purpose (or prohibiting any other use of them once created), the government would be approving the one practice in human embryo research that is widely condemned even by supporters of abortion rights: specially creating human embryos solely for the purpose of research that will kill them.

Therapeutic Cloning Should Not Be Banned

ARTHUR L. CAPLAN

In November 2001 an American biotech company named Advanced Cell Technology announced that it had produced a cloned human embryo that could, theoretically, develop into a newborn if implanted into a woman's uterus. In the controversy that followed the announcement, the distinction between therapeutic and reproductive cloning was often lost. According to Arthur L. Caplan, director of the Department of Medical Ethics at the University of Pennsylvania School of Medicine, this distinction is essential.

In the following selection, written in 2002, Caplan explains that in therapeutic cloning, the genetic material from a cell in an adult's body is fused with an egg cell from which the nucleus has been removed in order to create embryonic stem cells that have a genome identical to that of the donor. Reproductive cloning involves implanting the embryo produced by this process into the uterus of a surrogate mother; the embryo is then brought to full term in order to produce a living clone of the donor. Caplan argues that the five-day-old embryo produced in therapeutic cloning is not a human being and that the potential benefits of cloning research are too great not to proceed with this promising technology. The potential benefits include the development of therapies tailored to an individual's specific medical condition, the production of replacement organs, and cures or therapies for a variety of debilitating diseases.

I n the past two months [May and June 2002] I have talked with many people who have a keen interest in whether the Senate will decide to ban therapeutic cloning.[1] At a conference at a Philadelphia hospital, a large number of people, their bodies racked with tremors from Parkinson's disease, gathered to hear me speak about the ethics of stem-cell research. A few weeks earlier I had spoken to another group, many of whom were breathing with the assistance of oxygen tanks because they have a genetic disease, Alpha-1 antitrypsin deficiency, that destroys their lungs and livers. Earlier still I met with a group of parents whose children are paralyzed as a result of spinal cord injuries.

At each meeting I told the audience there was a good chance that the government would criminalize research that might find answers to their ailments if it required using cloned human embryos, on the grounds that research using such embryos is unethical. The audience members were incredulous. And well they should have been. A bizarre alliance of antiabortion religious zealots and technophobic neoconservatives along with a smattering of scientifically befuddled antibiotech progressives is pushing hard to insure that the Senate accords more moral concern to cloned embryos in dishes than it does to kids who can't walk and grandmothers who can't hold a fork or breathe.

The Opposition

Perhaps it should come as no surprise that George W. Bush and the House of Representatives have already taken the position that any research requiring the destruction of an embryo, cloned or otherwise, is wrong. This view derives

1. Although the U.S. House of Representatives voted to ban all human cloning in 1998, 2001, and 2003, divisions in the Senate prevented the proposals from passing each time. On March 31, 2005, state senators approved a bill allowing embryonic stem cell research in Massachusetts.

from the belief, held by many in the Republican camp, that personhood begins at conception, that embryos are people and that killing them to help other people is simply wrong. Although this view about the moral status of embryos does not square with what is known about them—science has shown that embryos require more than genes in order to develop, that not all embryos have the capacity to become a person and that not all conception begins a life—it at least has the virtue of moral clarity.

But aside from those who see embryos as tiny people such clarity of moral vision is absent among cloning opponents. Consider the views of [the chairman of the President's Council on Bioethics] Leon Kass, [the editor of the political magazine the *Weekly Standard*] William Kristol, [columnist] Charles Krauthammer and [author] Francis Fukuyama. Each says he opposes research involving the cloning of human embryos. Each has been pushing furiously in the media and in policy circles to make the case that nothing could be more morally heinous than harvesting stem cells from such embryos. And each says that his repugnance at the idea of cloning research has nothing to do with a religiously based view of what an embryo is.

The core of the case against cloning for cures is that it involves the creation, to quote the latest in a landslide of moral fulminations from Krauthammer, "of a human embryo for the sole purpose of using it for its parts . . . it will sanction the creation of an entire industry of embryo manufacture whose explicit purpose is . . . dismemberment for research." Sounds like a very grim business indeed—and some progressives, notably [authors] Jeremy Rifkin and Norman Mailer, have sounded a similar alarm as they have joined the anticloning crusade.

Secular Arguments Against Cloning

From the secular viewpoint, which Krauthammer and likeminded cloning opponents claim to hold, there is no evidence for the position that embryonic clones are persons or even potential persons. As a simple fact of science, embryos that reside in dishes are going nowhere. The potential to become anything requires a suitable environment. Talk of "dismemberment," which implicitly confers moral status on embryos, betrays the sort of faith-based thinking that Krauthammer says he wants to eschew. Equally ill-informed is the notion that equivalent medical benefits can be derived from research on adult stem cells; cloned embryonic stem cells have unique properties that cannot be duplicated.

The idea that women could be transformed into commercial egg farms also troubles Krauthammer, as well as some feminists and the Christian Medical Association. The CMA estimates that to make embryonic stem-cell cloning work, more than a billion eggs would have to be harvested. But fortunately for those hoping for cures, the CMA is wrong: Needed now for cloned embryonic stem-cell research are thousands of eggs, not billions. While cloning people is a long shot, cloning embryos is not, and it should be possible to get the research done either by paying women for their eggs or asking those who suffer from a disease, or who know someone they care about who has a disease, to donate them. Women are already selling and donating eggs to others who are trying to have babies. Women and men are also donating their kidneys, their bone marrow and portions of their livers to help others, at far greater risk to themselves than egg donation entails. And there is no reason that embryo splitting, the technique used today in animals, could not provide the requisite embryo and cloned stem-cell lines to treat all in need without a big increase in voluntary egg donation from women.

In addition to conjuring up the frightening but unrealistic image of women toiling in Dickensian embryo-cloning factories, those like Krauthammer, who would leave so many senior citizens unable to move their own bodies, offer two other moral thoughts. If we don't draw the line at cloning for cures, there will soon enough be a clone moving into your neighborhood; and besides, it is selfish and arrogant to seek to alter our own genetic makeup to live longer.

The Reality of Cloning

The reality is that cloning has a terrible track record in making embryos that can become fetuses, much less anything born alive. The most recent review of cloning research shows an 85 percent failure rate in getting cow embryos to develop into animals. And of those clones born alive, a significant percentage, more than a third, have serious life-threatening health problems. Cloned embryos have far less potential than embryos created the old-fashioned way, or even frozen embryos, of becoming anything except a ball of cells that can be tricked into becoming other cells that can cure diseases. Where Krauthammer sees cloned embryos as persons drawn and quartered for their organs, in reality there exists merely a construct of a cell that has no potential to become anything if it is kept safely in a dish and almost no potential to develop even if it is put into a womb. Indeed, current work on primate cloning has been so unproductive, which is to say none made to date, that there is a growing sentiment in scientific circles that human cloning for reproduction is impossible. The chance of anyone cloning a full-fledged human is almost nil, but in any case there is no reason that it cannot be stopped simply by banning the transfer of these embryos into wombs.

But should we really be manipulating our genes to try to cure diseases and live longer? Kass and Fukuyama, in various magazine pieces and books, say no—that it is selfish and arrogant indulgence at its worst. Humanity is not meant to play with its genes simply to live longer and better.

Now, it can be dangerous to try to change genes. One young man is dead because of an experiment in gene therapy at my medical school.[2] But the idea that genes are the

2. In 1999, eighteen-year-old Jesse Gelsinger died while undergoing treatment at the University of Pennsylvania's Institute for Human Gene Therapy.

defining essence of who we are and therefore cannot be touched or manipulated recalls the rantings of Gen. Jack D. Ripper in *Doctor Strangelove*, who wanted to preserve the integrity of his precious bodily fluids. There's nothing inherently morally wrong with trying to engineer cells, genes and even cloned embryos to repair diseases and terminal illnesses. Coming from those who type on computers, wear glasses, inject themselves with insulin, have had an organ transplant, who walk with crutches or artificial joints or who have used in vitro fertilization or neonatal intensive care to create their children, talk of the inviolate essence of human nature and repugnance at the "manufactured" posthuman is at best disingenuous.

The debate over human cloning and stem-cell research has not been one of this nation's finest moral hours. Pseudoscience, ideology and plain fearmongering have been much in evidence. If the discussions were merely academic, this would be merely unfortunate. They are not. The flimsy case against cloning for cures is being brought to the White House, the Senate and the American people as if the opponents hold the moral high ground. They don't. The sick and the dying do. The Senate must keep its moral priorities firmly in mind as the vote on banning therapeutic cloning draws close.

Chronology

1953
James Watson and Francis Crick's description of the double helix structure of DNA is published in *Nature* magazine.

1966
Marshall Niremberg, Heinrich Mathaei, and Severo Ochoa break the genetic code.

1969
James Shapiero and Jonathan Beckwith isolate the first gene.

1973
Stanley Cohen and Herbert Boyer produced the first recombinant DNA.

1976
Boyer and Robert Swanson found Genentech, a biotechnology company dedicated to developing and marketing products based on recombinant DNA technology.

1978
Genentech produces human insulin in genetically engineered *E. coli* bacteria; David M. Rorvik publishes the novel *In His Image: The Cloning of a Man*, which ignites a public debate on human cloning.

1980
In the case *Diamond v. Chakrabarty*, the U.S. Supreme Court rules that modified organisms can be patented.

1983

The U.S. Patent and Trademark Office grants patents for genetically modified plants.

1984

The first verified mammal cloning occurs when Steen Willadsen clones a sheep from embryo cells; the entire genome of the HIV virus is cloned and sequenced.

1986

The Environmental Protection Agency approves the first field tests of genetically engineered crops—tobacco plants.

1987

Frostban, a genetically altered bacterium that inhibits frost formation on crop plants, becomes the first engineered bacterium to be authorized for an outdoor test.

1988

"Oncomouse" becomes the first living mammal to be patented.

1990

The Human Genome Project, an international effort to map all the genes in the human body, is launched; the first federally approved gene therapy treatment is successfully performed on four-year-old Ashanti Desilva.

1992

The FDA declares that transgenic foods are "not inherently dangerous" and do not require special regulation.

1993

The FDA approves recombinant Bovine Growth Hormone (rBGH) for increased milk production in dairy cows.

1994

The Flavr Savr tomato becomes the first whole food produced through biotechnology to win FDA approval.

1997

Ian Wilmut at Scotland's Roslin Institute announces the birth of Dolly, the first mammal cloned from an adult cell.

1999

The first death directly related to gene therapy occurs when Jesse Gelsinger reacts negatively to an experimental infusion of a gene.

2001

First drafts of the human genome are released simultaneously by the Human Genome Project and Celera Genomics; U.S. scientists announce that babies have been born carrying the DNA of three parents: two women and a man; in his first address to the nation, President George W. Bush announces that he is limiting stem cell research using federal funds to existing stem cell lines.

2002

Clonaid, the research company formed by the Raelians, a UFO cult, claims that it has produced the first cloned human; Rice, the main food source for two-thirds of the world's population, becomes the first crop plant to have its genome decoded.

2003

Dolly, the cloned sheep, is euthanized after developing a progressive lung disease; the Human Genome Project is completed.

2004

South Korean researchers report the successful cloning of

thirty human embryos from which they were able to extract stem cells; American genetic engineers create a mouse that has enhanced muscle endurance.

2005

It is discovered that a thousand tons of banned, genetically engineered maize had inadvertently entered the European Union food chain over the previous four years.

Organizations to Contact

Biotechnology Industry Organization (BIO)
1225 Eye St. NW, Suite 400, Washington, DC 20005
(202) 962-9200
e-mail: info@bio.org • Web site: www.bio.org

BIO represents more than one thousand companies, academic institutions, and biotechnology centers. It advocates the industry's positions to elected officials and regulators, provides information about the industry's progress and contributions to quality of life, and informs political and public reaction to genetically modified foods.

Center for Bioethics and Human Dignity (CBHD)
2065 Half Day Rd., Bannockburn, IL 60015
(847) 317-8180 • fax: (847) 317-8101
e-mail: info@cbhd.org • Web site: www.cbhd.org

CBHD is a nonprofit group that provides a Christian perspective on biotechnology issues. It helps individuals and organizations address the pressing bioethical challenges of the day, including managed care, end-of-life treatment, genetic intervention, euthanasia and suicide, and reproductive technologies. It has published a number of books covering cloning, reproductive ethics, and stem cell research.

Center for Food Safety (CFS)
660 Pennsylvania Ave. SE, #302, Washington, DC 20003
(202) 547-9359 • fax: (202) 547-9429
e-mail: office@centerforfoodsafety.org
Web site: www.centerforfoodsafety.org

CFS is a nonprofit public interest and environmental advocacy membership organization established in 1997 by its sister organization, the International Center for Technology Assessment, for the purpose of challenging harmful food production technologies and promoting sustainable alternatives. CFS combines multiple tools and strategies in pursuing its goals, including litigation and legal petitions for rulemaking, legal support for various sustainable agriculture and food safety constituencies, public education, grassroots organizing, and media outreach.

Council for Biotechnology Information

1225 Eye St. NW, Suite 400, Washington, DC 20043-0380
(202) 467-6565
Web site: www.whybiotech.com

The Council for Biotechnology Information communicates science-based information about the benefits and safety of agricultural and food biotechnology. Its members are the leading biotechnology companies and trade associations. The council advocates for the continuation of biotechnology research and development governed by science-based regulatory systems to ensure that the products reaching the market are safe for people, animals, and the environment.

Council for Responsible Genetics (CRG)

5 Upland Rd., Suite 3, Cambridge, MA 02140
(617) 868-0870 • fax: (617) 491-5344
e-mail: crg@gene-watch.org • Web site: www.gene-watch.org

CRG is a nonprofit, nongovernmental organization that fosters public debate about the social, ethical, and environmental implications of genetic technologies. It works through the media and concerned citizens to distribute accurate information and represent the public interest on emerging issues in biotechnology. CRG publishes *GeneWatch*, America's only magazine dedicated to monitoring biotechnology's social, ethical, and environmental consequences.

Genetic Engineering Action Network (GEAN)

11 Ward St., Suite 200, Somerville, MA 02143
(617) 661-6626
e-mail: info@geaction.org • Web site: www.geaction.org

GEAN is a diverse network of grassroots activists, national and community nongovernmental organizations, farmer and farm advocacy groups, academics, and scientists working on the myriad issues surrounding biotechnology. GEAN offers technical support and ongoing organizing assistance, for groups working on genetic engineering issues.

Genetic Resources Action International (GRAIN)
Girona 25, pral., E-08010, Barcelona, Spain
(34) 933-011381 • fax: (34) 933-011627
e-mail: grain@grain.org • Web site: www.grain.org

GRAIN is an international nongovernmental organization that promotes the sustainable management and use of agricultural biodiversity. GRAIN actively monitors, researches, and lobbies against pressures that undermine the rights of farmers and other local communities to use and benefit from biodiversity and advocates for building up mechanisms that enhance community control over local genetic resources and their associated knowledge. The organization publishes a quarterly magazine called *Seedling*.

Gene Watch UK
The Mill House, Manchester Rd., Tideswell, Buxton, Derbyshire, SK17 8LN, United Kingdom
(44) 1298-871898 • fax: (44) 1298-972531
e-mail: mail@genewatch.org • Web site: www.genewatch.org

The aims of Gene Watch are to ensure that genetic technologies are developed and used in the public interest, and in a way that promotes human health, protects the environment, and respects human rights and the interests of animals. Gene Watch is a nonprofit group that monitors developments in genetic technologies, from genetically modified crops and foods to the genetic testing of humans; aims to increase public understanding of genetic technologies; and carries out research about their impact.

International Centre for Genetic Engineering and Biotechnology (ICGEB)
AREA Science Park, Padriciano 99, 34012 Trieste, Italy
(39) 040-37571
e-mail: icgeb@icgeb.org • Web site: www.icgeb.org

ICGEB promotes the safe use of biotechnology. It conducts innovative research in life sciences for the benefit of developing countries, strengthening the research capability of its member states through training programs, funding, and advisory services. ICGEB works to advance knowledge in molecular biology and apply the latest biotechnology techniques in the fields of public health, energy production, industrial production, nutrition, and environmental protection.

Books

Miguel A. Altieri, *Genetic Engineering in Agriculture: The Myths, Environmental Risks, and Alternatives.* Oakland: Food First, 2004.

British Medical Association, *Biotechnology, Weapons and Humanity.* London: BMJ Bookshop, 1999.

John P. Burgess, *In Whose Image? Faith, Science and the New Genetics.* Louisville, KY: Geneva 1998.

Ronald Cole-Turner, ed., *Beyond Cloning: Religion and the Remaking of Humanity.* Harrisburg, PA: Trinity International, 2001.

Donald Conroy, ed., *Earth at Risk: An Environmental Dialogue Between Religion and Science.* New York: Humanity, 2000.

Celia Deane-Drummond, *Theology and Biotechnology: Implications for a New Science.* London: Geoffrey Chapman, 1997.

Scott Eastham, *Biotech Time-Bomb: How Genetic Engineering Could Irreversibly Change Our World.* Auckland, NZ: RSVP, 2003.

Maitland A. Edey and Donald C. Johanson, *Blueprints: Solving the Mystery of Evolution.* Boston: Little, Brown, 1989.

John H. Evans, *Playing God? Human Genetic Engineering and the Rationalization of Public Bioethical Debate.* Chicago: University of Chicago Press, 2002.

Nina Fedoroff and Nancy Marie Brown, *Mendel in the Kitchen:*

Scientists' View of Genetically Modified Food. Washington, DC: National Academies, 2004.

John Harris, *Clones, Genes and Immortality: Ethics and Genetics.* Oxford: Oxford University Press, 1998.

Kathleen Hart, *Eating in the Dark: America's Experiment with Genetically Engineered Food.* New York: Pantheon, 2002.

Suzanne Holland, Karen Lebacqz, and Laurie Zoloth, eds., *The Human Embryonic Stem Cell Debate: Science, Ethics, and Public Policy.* Cambridge, MA: MIT Press, 2001.

Philip Kitcher, *The Lives to Come: The Genetic Revolution and Human Possibilities.* New York: Simon & Schuster, 1996.

Sheldon Krimsky and Peter Shorett, eds., *Rights and Liberties in the Biotech Age: Why We Need a Genetic Bill of Rights.* New York: Rowman & Littlefield, 2005.

Marc Lappe and Britt Bailey, eds., *Engineering the Farm: The Social and Ethical Aspects of Agricultural Biotechnology.* Covelo, CA: Island, 2002.

Jeff Lyon and Peter Gorner, *Altered Fates: Gene Therapy and the Retooling of Human Life.* New York: W.W. Norton, 1995.

Belinda Martineau, *First Fruit: The Creation of the Flavr Savr Tomato and the Birth of Genetically Engineered Food.* New York: McGraw-Hill, 2001.

Bill McKibben, *Enough: Genetic Engineering and the End of Human Nature.* London: Bloomsbury, 2003.

Stephen Nottingham, *Eat Your Genes: How Genetically Modified Food Is Entering Our Diet.* New York: Zed, 2003.

Paul Pechan and Gert de Vries, *Genes on the Menu: Facts for Knowledge-Based Decisions.* London: Springer, 2005.

Gregory E. Pence, ed., *Flesh of My Flesh: The Ethics of Cloning Humans*. New York: Rowman & Littlefield, 1998.

———, *Who's Afraid of Human Cloning?* New York: Rowman & Littlefield, 1998.

James Peterson, *Genetic Turning Points: The Ethics of Human Genetic Intervention*. Grand Rapids, MI: Eerdmans, 2001.

Karen Peterson-Lyer, *Designer Children: Reconciling Genetic Technology, Feminism, and Christian Faith*. Cleveland, OH: Pilgrim, 2004.

President's Council on Bioethics, *Human Cloning and Human Dignity*. New York: Public Affairs, 2002.

Peter Pringle, *Food, Inc.: Mendel to Monsanto—The Promises and Perils of the Biotech Harvest*. New York: Simon & Schuster, 2003.

Michael Reiss and Roger Straughan, *Improving Nature? The Science and Ethics of Genetic Engineering*. New York: Cambridge University Press, 1996.

Jeremy Rifkin, *The Biotech Century: Harnessing the Gene and Remaking the World*. New York: Jeremy P. Tarcher/ Putnam, 1998.

Jane Rissler and Margaret Mellon, *The Ecological Risks of Engineered Crops*. Cambridge, MA: MIT Press, 1996.

Michael Ruse and Aryne Sheppard, eds., *Cloning: Responsible Science or Technomadness?* Amherst, MA: Prometheus, 2001.

Vandana Shiva, *Biopiracy: The Plunder of Nature and Knowledge*. Boston: South End, 1997.

Lee M. Silver, *Remaking Eden: Cloning, Genetic Engineering and the Future of Humankind?* New York: Avon, 1997.

C. Neal Stewart, *Genetically Modified Planet: Environmental Impacts of Genetically Engineered Plants*. Oxford: Oxford University Press, 2004.

Gregory Stock and John Campbell, eds., *Engineering the Human Germline: An Exploration of the Science and Ethics of Altering the Genes We Pass to Our Children*. Oxford: Oxford University Press, 2000.

Periodicals

Brian Alexander, "(You)2," *Wired*, February 2001.

David Barboza, "As Biotech Crops Multiply, Consumers Get Little Choice," *New York Times*, June 10, 2001.

Rowan Hooper, "The Radical Route to a Longer Life," *New Scientist*, May 2005.

Gina Kolata, "Who Owns Your Genes?" *New York Times*, May 15, 2000.

Andrew Pollack, "No Foolproof Way Is Seen to Contain Altered Genes," *New York Times*, January 21, 2004.

Michael Pollan, "Playing God in the Garden," *New York Times*, October 25, 1998.

David Quist and Ignacio H. Chapela, "Transgenic DNA Introgressed Into Traditional Maize Landraces in Oaxaca, Mexico," *Nature*, November 2001.

Adam Rogers, "The Mice That Roar," *Newsweek*, August 3, 1998.

David Shenk, "Biocapitalism: What Price the Genetic Revolution?" *Harper's Magazine*, December 1997.

Michael Shermer, "Skeptic: I, Clone," *Scientific American*, April 2003.

Internet Sources

Ralph Brave, "Governing the Genome," 2001. www.thenation .com/doc.mhtml?i=20011210&s=brave#.

Christian Aid, "International Policy Briefings: Biotechnology and Genetically Modified Organisms," 2000. www.christ ian-aid.org.uk/indepth/0001biot/biotech.htm.

Kristi Coale, "Mutant Food," 2000. http://dir.salon.com/news /feature/2000/01/12/food/index.html.

Martha L. Crouch, "How the Terminator Terminates: An Explanation for the Non-Scientist of a Remarkable Patent for Killing Second Generation Seeds of Crop Plants," 1998. www.edmonds-institute.org/crouch.html.

Marcy Darnovsky, "The New Eugenics: The Case Against Genetically Modified Humans," 2000. http://members.tri pod.com/~ngin/technoeugenic.htm.

Mark Dowie, "Gods and Monsters," 2004. www.motherjones. com/news/feature/2004/01/12_401.html.

Ron Epstein, "Ethical Dangers of Genetic Engineering," 1999. www.greens.org/s-r/20/20-01.html.

Greenpeace USA, "Pharm Crops: A Food Accident Waiting to Happen," 2001. www.greenpeace.org/usa/press/ reports/pharm-crops-a-food-accident.

Richard Hayes, "The Politics of Genetically Engineered Humans," 2000. www.loka.org/alerts/loka.7.2.txt.

Rachel Massey, "Engineering Humans," 2001. www.rachel. org/search/index.cfm?St=1.

Arpad Pusztai, "Genetically Modified Foods: Are They a Risk to Human/Animal Health?" 2001. www.actionbio science.org/biotech/pusztai.html#Primer.

Jeremy Rifkin, "Now for GM Weapons," 2001. www.guardian. co.uk/comment/story/0,,558767,00.html.

Mark Sagoff, "Patented Genes: An Ethical Appraisal," 1998. www.issues.org/issues/14.3/sagoff.htm.

Index

surrogate cells, 105
Swanson, Robert, 13
synchronicity, 107

Takamine, Jokichi, 111
Tangier disease, 132
Taylor, Michael, 119
Tay-Sachs screening, 127
technological view, of cloning,
194–95
"terminator" technology, 24
testing, 138–39, 171
test-tube baby, 172
Texas cattle ranchers, 57
therapeutic cloning, 19
therapy, restorative stem cell,
156
Third World, 94
Thomson, James, 210
Tipton, Sean, 168
tissue culturing, 35
tobacco, pest-resistant, 31
tobacco plants, 29, 93
tomatoes
engineered, 23, 24, 38
flounder genes inserted into,
29, 93
toxins, 63
trade, 41, 46–47
transgenic crops, 30, 31
transplantation, 94, 184
Treflan (Rival), 74, 79
trust, public, 41, 44
Tsipis, Judith, 128, 133
Tunisia, rBGH trials in, 90
twins, monozygotic, 178, 180

umbilical cords, 146
United Kingdom, 156
United States, 99–100
University of Illinois, 117, 121

Upjohn, 87
utility requirement (law),
110–11, 113

vaccines, 39, 160
Van Aker, Rene, 79
Varmus, Harold, 136, 137, 139,
140, 141, 153
veal, 87–88
vectors, 135, 138
vegetarian practices, 58
"veggie libel" laws, 57
Venter, Craig, 15, 16, 17, 126,
130, 158
viruses, 31–32, 135

Walters, LeRoy, 138
Waters, Alice, 55
Watson, James, 13, 16, 130,
157, 158
weeds, resistant, 31, 32, 36
Weldon, Dave, 154, 207
Wilmut, Ian, 17, 104, 106, 107,
108, 175
Wilson, Jim, 138, 139, 140, 141,
143
wines, sulfite label on, 58
Winfrey, Oprah, 57
Wivel, Nelson, 139
women's liberation, 195
World Resources Institute, 94
World Trade Organization, 37

yams, 67, 69
yeast, patent for, 111

Zakreski, Terry J., 72, 73
Zambia, rBGH trials in, 90
Zavos, Panayiotis, 18, 168
Zimbabwe, rBGH trials in, 90
Zitner, A., 209